Hop to It

A Guide to Training Your Pet Rabbit

Samantha Hunter

With Photographs by Dennis Colwell

And a special chapter on
Keeping Your Bunny Healthy
by Petra Burgmann, DVM

Consulting Editor: Lucia Vriends-Parent

BARRON'S

All inquiries should be addressed to:
Barron's Educational Series, Inc.
250 Wireless Boulevard
Hauppauge, NY 11788

Library of Congress Catalog Card Number 90–25342

International Standard Book Number 0-8120-4551-3

Library of Congress Cataloging-in-Publication Data

Hunter, Samantha.
    Hop to it: a guide to training your pet rabbit / Samantha
    Hunter; with photographs by Dennis Colwell.
        p.   cm.
    Includes bibliographical references and index.
    ISBN 0-8120-4551-3
    1. Rabbits—Training.   2. Rabbits. I. Title.
SF453.H86   1991   90-25342
636′.9322—dc20   CIP

PRINTED IN HONG KONG

6 7 8   4900   13

Note of Warning

This book deals with the keeping and care of rabbits as pets. In working with these animals, you may occasionally sustain minor scratches or bites. Have such wounds treated by a doctor at once.

As a result of unhygienic living conditions, rabbits can have mites and other external parasites, some of which can be transmitted to humans or to pet animals, including cats and dogs. Have the infested rabbit treated by a veterinarian at once (see page 67), and go to the doctor yourself at the slightest suspicion that you may be harboring one of these pests. When buying a rabbit, be sure to look for the signs of parasite infestation.

Rabbits must be watched very carefully during the necessary and regular exercise period in the house. To avoid life-threatening accidents, be particularly careful that your pet does not gnaw on any electrical wires.

Photo Credits
Gräfe and Unzer: Cover (photographer, Monika Wegler); page 5, top right; page 36.

FOR WOODSTOCK & JOHN PETER MACKENZIE
for all the right reasons

Acknowledgments

I would like to state my appreciation for some of the people who enthusiastically shared database information that is difficult to uncover. They were of immense help in enabling me to understand the demographics of the bunnyworld: David Monk, *Facts Canada*; Allison Brown, Canadian National Exhibition; Irene Clark, Founder, Dominion Rabbit & Cavey Breeders Association; and Nancy Cross, Judge, Show Rabbits.

Friends who contributed to this publication with their encouragement and assistance are Arlene and Heather Crewe. They provided me with every available printed word about rabbits.

Friends who consented to be photgraphed—with their pet rabbits: Lori and Kevin Sweeting, Gisela Kozlovskis, Julie Kellman.

Special thanks are due Peter Buchanan who bred Woodstock and provided the last line in this book. He gives unstintingly of his formidable knowledge about rabbits to anyone who simply asks.

Special thanks go to Cathy and Ron Lee who placed their rabbits Smokey and Benji in my hands to bunnysit—thereby triggering the chain of events that led to this publication.

There is no way to express my gratitude to Peter MacKenzie, who placed Woodstock in my arms and prodded and nurtured me in the completion of this project. This book would still be a dream without his tenacity.

Finally, my editor, Don Reis, and the dedicated staff at Barron's.

Contents

What kind of a bunny are you?

Preface

This book is based on years of exposure to rabbits—my own pet, of course, as well as those I have met through friends, pet associations, and breeders. As a result of this exposure, I have developed an ongoing curiosity about these loveable animals. The more I have learned, the more fascinated I have become!

As a child, I was enthralled when the magician pulled a rabbit out of his hat and the children played with it afterward. In retrospect, this was undoubtedly my very first exposure to rabbits. As an adult, I was equally enthralled by the magnificent work of literature entitled *Watership Down.* Truly an inspired creation, its message is irresistible.

Even at that time, however, I had no idea I would be the proud owner of "Woodstock," the rambunctious buck who taught me so much about bunny ownership.

This book demystifies the "hare-raising" experiences of the first-time bunny owner. Despite prior knowledge about different breeds, many helpful hints from friends, tips from breeders, and other readily available information, it will all finally come down to the moment when you are alone with your new pet. I hope that I succeed in preparing you for that moment—and the years that follow.

The acknowledgments indicate the support I had from a number of wonderful people. Without their prodding I would never have met my Woodstock, and without them he might never have survived my well-intentioned but sometimes bizarre training and handling techniques.

Woodstock is two years old and thriving. He has been on national TV in Canada and is now auditioning for commercials. If he could put his paw print on this Preface, it would probably be for the ultimate communication between pet bunny and bunny owner.

Samantha Hunter
Spring, 1991

Chapter 1

So, You're Thinking About Buying a Bunny

Before you even consider adopting a bunny (unless it's already too late), there are a few facts you should understand about rabbits as pets. For example, would it surprise you to know. . .

- That there are probably as many breeds of rabbits as there are of dogs?
- That rabbits, even in the wild, have an advanced social structure?
- That rabbits relate to strangers as well as, or better than, other domesticated animals?
- That the organic structure of rabbits is similar to our own, which is one reason why they are a preferred laboratory species?
- That rabbits are as emotionally sensitive as dogs and cats?
- That rabbits have an affinity for children and senior citizens and are being used in North America for communication therapy in hospitals, nursing homes, and facilities for the mentally retarded?

- That rabbits have been known to mankind as a pet since the early 1600s?

Bunny Ownership

It is predicted that rabbits will become the "Pet of the Future." Why?

- They don't bark, meow, or make other "peace-disturbing" noises.
- They require nominal veterinary care and their feeding and housing are easier on the household budget than other domestic pets.
- They can maintain themselves over a long weekend without trauma, given clean housing, adequate food, and fresh water.
- They don't smell—they are self-cleaning, provided their housing is kept clean.
- They don't bite, unless abused or misunderstood.
- They are docile by nature (some breeds have been bred to enhance this particular trait).

- They are surprisingly affectionate when properly raised and nurtured.
- Many individuals with mild allergies can live comfortably with a rabbit.
- Studies indicate that rabbits are not known to transmit diseases to humans.
- They make good traveling companions.

These are some of the positives for rabbits as household pets. As word of these virtues spreads, more people are becoming interested in rabbits as pets and discovering their most recent surprising trait: *They are more trainable than you could possibly imagine!*

That trait is what this book is all about—training rabbits.

Bunny Research

If you take pet ownership seriously, you may have done some research on rabbits. There are some excellent publications available to you, such as Monika Wegler's book entitled *Rabbits* and Lucia Vriends-Parent's *New Rabbit Handbook* (see page 75). Books like these were invaluable to me during my early days with Woodstock. They contain a wealth of information on care, housing, nutrition, and health. In conjunction with your veterinarian's advice, a good pet owner's manual can become the bible for your pet's well-being. Each time you refer to it, you will find something else new or forgotten.

However, none of the publications I read P.T.W. (Prior to Woodstock) prepared me for the long-term living relationship I was determined to have with my trained, "user-friendly" bunny.

Accepting a pet into your home makes you totally responsible for its health and well-being for the duration of its lifespan. For rabbits, this could be up to a decade—and I'm sure there are some longer-lived exceptions in the *Guiness Book of World Records*. But domesticated animals didn't ask to be born or live with humans, which dictates Bunny Rules I and II:

When you own a bunny, you have a sensitive animal in captivity. While bred in captivity, the animal still shares centuries of traits inherited from its wild ancestors, which we recognize as instincts. Although the rabbit's natural instincts have been altered by crossbreeding to create traits more suitable to a pet, that does not mean that these instincts have disappeared! For example, dogs will still circle before they lie down, a trait that originated with their wild ancestors who circled in high grasses to clear a bed. Cats will always crouch, stalk, and pounce. And rabbits will always do rabbity things, most of which are described for you in this book.

Introducing Bunny Rule I

For Woodstock, I equate this rule with the Country/Western song,

The very pleasant result of a cross between a Netherlands dwarf and a Netherlands lop.

"Walk a Mile in my Shoes." If you cannot, emotionally, hop in a rabbit's paws for about five to ten years, leave the adorable creature for a pet owner who can. The dependency of bunnies on their owners cannot be overstressed.

Truly unique and delightful animals, rabbits will respond best on a long-term basis to trust-training (I'm O.K.—you're O.K.). If you have the patience of Job, the support of other family members, and time to spend with your bunny on a regular basis, you will be astounded at the results you can achieve. Trust-training, which is the basis of this book, is not a short-term project. With an investment from you of about one to two hours a day, it will take at least six months. Regardless of rabbit breed,

Though they are obviously from different litters, these two bucks live together in perfect harmony.

it is unlikely to take longer than nine months.

Familiar methods of domestic-pet animal training include food motivation—deprivation or reward; and activity motivation—confinement or freedom. These training methods seemed inappropriate to me for a pet as sensitive as a bunny and dictates Bunny Rule II.

To understand Rule II, it may help to establish the difference between the rabbit as a household pet and a "user-friendly bunny." *All* rabbits raised in captivity are basically tame and can be completely housebroken. You don't need to invest the time in trust-training to have a perfectly satisfactory household pet. But if you want to enjoy the full potential of your rabbit and want your pet to have the maximum freedom of your home,

nurturing must be broadened to include trust-training.

Introducing Bunny Rule II

Establish what you wish to accomplish with your rabbit. Do you simply want an easy-to-care-for household pet or do you want the challenge and rewards of a user-friendly bunny that will delight your friends, relatives, and guests and provide unlimited hours of warmth, affection, and comedy?

Having established your feelings about Bunny Rules I and II, you will find information in this book that will enhance your ability to grasp the nature of rabbits as pets, ensure their well-being, and stimulate their responses to training.

Left: Woodstock, in the basket, is a mixed-breed lop (English and Meissner). His masked friend is a mixed brood calico.

A Netherlands dwarf—the smallest of all rabbit breeds and the one that comes in the most color combinations.

Chapter 2
Choosing Your Bunny

My Choice

There he was! A good-size bunny at eleven weeks old who had been too old to be chosen at Easter. A minilop with chocolate-brown floppy ears and eye markings to match, soft brown eyes and the rest pure white (or so I thought until he matured). I was simply window shopping, but he was such a big baby that I asked the breeder to bring him out of his cage. The next thing I knew, he had been handed to me and my friend said "That's it, let's go!" I've never been too sure since whether either of us, the bunny or me, had a choice. Of course I felt sorry for the Easter bunny bandit with the brown face mask who couldn't find a home, so what else could I do? My friend and the breeder looked so pleased with themselves it made me nervous— and with good cause, as it was to develop on the homebound trip. (See Transporting Your Rabbit Home, page 17.)

Your Choice

I strongly recommend that the selection of your bunny be based upon your own personal research. As pre- viously mentioned, there are many breeds. Conversations with breeders, rabbit association members, veterinarians, and friends helped me to make my choice. Books are another excellent research source to provide you with an understanding of breeds and their characteristics. *The New Rabbit Handbook,* for example, has full-color photographs and brief descriptions of the most popular rabbit breeds (see page 75).

Sources

Show breeders frequently retain rabbits that are a little short of show-stock standards for sale to customers seeking a pet. Breeders are usually cautious about not releasing a baby bunny until it is six to eight weeks of age, is in good health, and has a good start. Also, when selecting a pet from a breeder, you will be able to discover its lineage.

Pet shops are an obvious source, but when acquiring a rabbit from a pet shop I would request the name of the breeder. Follow up with a phone call to get information about the lineage and breed.

Newspaper ads may offer rabbits that have been bred in a home environment. Such offerings are probably worth following up with a personal interview.

The Humane Society accepts homeless rabbits given up when they become a little more mature and cease to be tiny and cute. These rabbits have had some exposure to home life and are quite receptive to someone who cares for them.

If you find an appealing adolescent, you need have no fear that it has become too set in its ways. My experience in researching rabbit training indicates that there is no known learning limit for a rabbit. Woodstock is still open to new commands, as was my friend's nine-year-old rabbit, Smokey.

Multiple Bunnies

I have, on occasion, observed that families with two children often purchase two rabbits. If the children were male and female, the parents tended to purchase a male and female bunny. The obvious is inevitable, so it is important to understand that in a short time your rabbits will reach sexual maturity. (See Fixing Your Bunny, page 57.) Two male rabbits tend toward serious aggression when they reach maturity. Although less aggressive, two unrelated females will also fight. Two rabbits means double the training, as it must be done on an individual basis. If the intent was for each child to have his or her own pet, it is unnecessary as rabbits will adopt everyone in the family equally. Like any other animal, they tend to follow the person who feeds them. Having everyone share in this task eliminates any favoritism. Finally, one bunny will be much more affectionate and dependent upon its human family.

Some Popular Rabbit Breeds

Alaska	English lop	New Zealand Black
American	English spot	New Zealand Red
American checkered giant	Flemish giant (or Patagonian)	New Zealand White
Angora	Florida white	Palomino
Belgian Hare	French lop	Polish
Van beveren	Harlequin	Rex
Californian	Havana	Rhinelander
Chinchilla	Himalayan	Satin
American chinchilla	Lotharinger	Silver fox
American giant chinchilla	Marten	Silvers
Chinchilla giganta	Netherlands dwarf	Tan
Dutch	Netherlands dwarf lop	Thueringer
		Viennese

Left: Gisela's choice—a brownish gray Netherlands dwarf.
Right: Lori's choice—a gray Netherlands dwarf lop.

Left: Julie's choice—a black-and-white mixed breed.
Right: My choice.

Chapter 3
Taking Your Bunny Home

Transportation

The size of a rabbit's cage should be dictated by the size of the rabbit's anticipated growth, but a rabbit cage can never be too large. If the cage is too large for the back seat of your car, but will fit in the trunk, purchase a travel cage as well for the occasion. It can be put on the back seat with the bunny inside and will come in very handy later. *Never,* ever put a rabbit, baby or mature, in a cage in a trunk!

If the rabbit cage is too large for the back seat and you decide not to buy a travel cage, your pet should either be held in your arms or on your lap in an open cardboard box. Only one person should hold your pet on the way home, and the windows should be closed. A rabbit can sense the open space and this, combined with the motion of the car, may cause it to go into a mad scramble—which can be very scary this early in your bunny ownership. Avoid loud noises and keep the car radio low or off, particularly if your new pet has spent his first six to eight weeks in a hutch. *Do not take any detours* on the way home!

If the pet is to be a family bunny, you should have collectively decided on a name in advance. The person responsible for comforting the rabbit on the trip home should talk constantly to it in a low tone of voice, using the chosen name as frequently as possible. Do not change names—even this early, it can confuse your pet—and do not use endearing names until much later in the training. Constant endearments like cutey or sweetie may cause your pet to believe that is its name.

Anyone who is going to handle and reassure the pet en route should be forewarned that the animal is very likely to urinate from nervousness. Woodstock was true to form. The reason that I mentioned detours is that we made a big mistake in taking him to see some friends first. We finally got the poor little rascal home after a four-hour drive. When I found out later that we had done just about everything you should never do to a baby bunny, I went on an immediate guilt trip.

A large wire cage with a removable bottom is recommended as permanent housing. A small wire cage may be used as temporary housing and on long trips. A small vinyl case is handy for short trips.

Welcome Home!

Before you bring your rabbit home, decide where you are going to house your pet on a long-term basis. Upon arrival at home, place the cage in its permanent location, put in the recommended quantity of food for the appropriate time of day, and provide ample fresh water. If someone else is comforting the pet by stroking, holding, and speaking softly to it while you are setting up the housing, this person should settle the bunny in by either putting it on the floor or in its cage. See Chapter 5, page 26 for ways of accomplishing this quickly and painlessly for all parties.

The next most important thing to do is to *leave your pet bunny alone!* It is crucial that the bunny has time to get over the trauma of change, the fact that it is no longer with others of its species, and to adjust to a strange new cage and a totally new environment with no familiar smells. At this point, bunnies don't need strange people hauling them out of homes which they haven't even adopted yet—or even petting them. This will only confuse and frighten them.

It may be difficult to restrain children who want to enjoy their cuddly pet immediately. Remember that children have little comprehension of pet training unless it is instilled in them and reinforced by an adult. Leaving the bunny alone at this critical time is the first and most important step toward a trust-training program for a truly user-friendly bunny. Do not even approach the cage for the first three days except to feed and water your pet. I also suggest that you not clean the cage for three days so that your bunny can quickly establish the cage as his home by scent.

It is common knowledge that rabbits urinate and defecate as far away from their food as possible, so when you first clean the cage you should be able to identify the area staked out as a bathroom. This is normally the left or right back corner of the cage. There will be changes from time to time in the early stages before your bunny settles down. Feeding and housing equipment are admirably covered in other rabbit books, but I have addressed housing from a training perspective in Chapter 7, "Housekeeping and Grooming."

Housing

The best housing I have found is a sizeable cage with a bottom drawer. This permits cleaning in the early stages without reaching in or disturbing the cage or the rabbit. Several publications I read before owning

Take a small travel cage with you whenever you and your bunny go for an outing.

Woodstock indicated that "bedding" is a necessary requirement and suggested soft blankets or carpeting. Perhaps because Woodstock was born and weaned in a wire cage, he didn't seem to give a hoot about indoor carpeting or blankets. When they were placed in his cage he simply tossed them into the far corner and ignored them and was quite content to lie on the wire floor over the drawer. When I was later told by my veterinarian that the chewing of blankets and/or carpeting can create the equivalent of a cat's hairballs in a rabbit's stomach, I was pleased that Woodstock had Spartan taste in decor. We compromised on half pieces of clean towels that he pushes around and uses to catch whatever feces he needs to redigest. (See the special chapter by Dr. Burgmann on veterinarian care for rabbits, pages 61–71.)

We put a block of wood in Woodstock's cage for him to chew on. This helped to keep his teeth in good condition. Later, we substituted fresh small tree branches free of insecticides. If you should follow suit, be prepared to hear a lot of crashing around late at night. That was always when Woodstock liked to move his furniture around.

Chapter 4

Bunnyproofing Your Home

The most important thing is to understand rabbitry! For some reason, unknown and mysterious to me, rabbits like electrical wiring and telephone cords, and their more sophisticated palates lean toward coaxial cables. No one seems to be able to explain why they never seem to get a shock through their bunny teeth. Thank goodness I had a friendly telephone lineman because Woodstock made short work of my new phone lines. It didn't help that I had two 18-foot cords on two phones in two different rooms and lots of computer coaxial cable. It doesn't take a mental genius to figure out that you can't keep getting free phone cords from your friendly lineman in return for coffee forever, so I had to figure out a way to "bunnyproof" my home. Here are some things you can do.

Carpeting

Cut four mats from leftover carpeting and place them in the four corners of every room your bunny will have access to. These corners will be where your bunny will urinate to mark the boundaries of its domain. It won't be long before you will be able to remove them.

Stereo Equipment

Mount hooks or use nails on the backs of the cabinets of your stereo equipment. Gather all the wires together and secure them with tape or rubber bands and hang them from the hooks so that they are out of reach when your pet is standing on its back legs and stretched upward. In Woodstock's case, this is a good two and a half feet (12 cm).

Blocking Areas

With a little ingenuity you can block off forbidden areas. For example, floor speakers can be positioned to block the back of your stereo equipment. We used dried flower arrangements in tall vases to barricade strategic wiring for our tropical fish tank. These arrangements have eye appeal at floor level and have effectively inhibited Woodstock's desire to investigate behind them. Of course, we

Discourage your pet's interest in wiring. Better still, avoid exposed wiring in free play areas.

had to stop him from eating the barricade!

Shortening Wires

We shortened the electrical wiring on all lamps that were at Woodstock's level before letting him loose. This was easily done by gathering the excess wire and tucking it under the lamp base. Once he was trained that this was a "no-no" we didn't have to bother with it again—except when I am on the phone too long. (It's uncanny how animals know when you can't discipline them.)

Doors

Be certain you know the area you are offering your bunny before you set your pet free. It may change depending on your schedule or the time of day. We close all the doors along the hall in our apartment. This creates a run for Woodstock and gives him the freedom of the living room,

dining room, solarium, and kitchen. As your pet matures and starts following you around, be careful not to step on it or catch it in a door. Make sure that everyone is aware of these dangers. No one should ever open a closed door suddenly.

Cooking

If your pet is loose while you are cooking, be prepared for it to get underfoot or become very agitated and to start circling your feet or pawing at your legs for attention. You will have to stop what you are doing and give it some attention. When your rabbit is underfoot, be careful not to trip over it. Be especially careful at the stove—I almost dropped a scalding pot of spaghetti on Woodstock.

Bedrooms

Discourage allowing your pet access to bedrooms if you can, because bunnies like to hide under beds. Unless you have long arms or an unusual rapport with your pet, you will spend a lot of time face down trying to retrieve the little rascal.

Furniture

Don't be ready to discipline too quickly. Just when I would think Woodstock was going to take a bite out of a piece of furniture, I'd find out he was only "chinning" it. Woodstock has never taken a bite out of anything made of wood, contrary to what I was warned about. I attribute this to two things: a block of wood in his cage to chew on and his training commands (see Chapter 9). However, I have to admit that he has taken a bite out of a friend's leather briefcase, which I tried to explain away as a lovebite. I found this very funny until he repeated this performance on mine.

Plants

I let Woodstock explore the plant life in our apartment and there was quite a bit. Having introduced him to parsley, carrots, mint, and dill at the age of 20 weeks, he seemed to have developed a more sophisticated palate and spent most of his time simply "chinning" the plants.

Avoid poisonous plants, including daffodil, mistletoe, yew, hyacinth, narcissus, oleander, primrose, wax plant (*Hoya earnosa*), nux vomica, periwinkle (*vinca minor*), all Dieffenbachia species, and all plants of the nightshade family.

Sprays

There are a number of repellent sprays available. They are mostly manufactured for dogs and cats, but cat sprays seem to be effective for rabbits. These sprays can be invaluable in housebreaking. Most can be used on furniture and carpeting without concern. I would advise caution if a pet-store owner is hesitant when you ask if you can use it for a rabbit. Consult a breeder. Also, you should be careful if you have an infant at the crawling stage.

The most effective "bunnyproofing" you can do is training. Commands stop Woodstock from doing anything destructive and his only discipline is by voice. That is, of course, if I'm in the same room to see what he's up to. Try to remember that rabbits will always do rabbity things, but that they are less destructive and more easily trained than cats.

Chapter 5

Your Bunny's First Outing

Preparations

You should be talking to your pet the first week, but don't expect any miracles. Sit in front of the cage and place your palms upright on the wires. Using a soft tone, repeat warm phrases such as "You're a good boy, Woodstock." "Bunny-short" phrases *always* end with your bunny's name. This begins your pet's comprehension of the trust it can place in your handling and training. To create a user-friendly bunny, you must continue sitting in front of the cage and talking to it, even after your pet has had its first successful outing.

After a few days of bunny sitting, you will observe a lack of distress and, perhaps, even a show of interest in you. Your bunny may approach and sniff at your hand. When this happens, you are ready for the first outing. You must now establish *who* is willing to take responsibility for the rabbit's ongoing training. However, it must be understood that the person charged with the responsibility of training the user-friendly bunny needs a strong support system. In

some respects, it may actually be easier if you are on your own. This has drawbacks, too, as there are several things that take much longer to accomplish without a helping hand.

For example, try singlehandedly putting a harness on a strong rabbit, or checking its teeth, or putting it in a car, or rescuing it from a predator. A single trainer means that there is less likelihood of conflicting instructions, but also that there is less support and sharing of responsibility. If you are a single bunny parent, you can't help but be on your own. However, if there is even one other person in your household who will be exposed to your rabbit, he or she should be involved. For families, the person who will ultimately be responsible for the pet's training must be elected, and ongoing support for him or her should be assured.

The person in charge of the animal's training needs to understand the "rejection syndrome." The closer your bunny comes to you, the more it will ignore you and the more affectionate it will act toward others— even though you are the one who feeds it, trains it, and suffers agonies over its health and well-being. And the better behaved your pet is toward others, the more it will act up or ignore you. You'll know you have made the grade as a trainer if your rabbit comes streaking toward you when frightened or when it starts following you around the house. The warmer your bunny is toward others, the better you are doing. It won't take too long before you are able to call your pet by name and get an immediate response.

Once elected, the responsible individual must have *full support* from every household member during the training period. Everyone must use the vocabulary selected by the trainer and *nothing else.* Supportive household members must understand "bunny possession," which means simply that rabbits know no master and will adopt each household member as their family. Given time they will explore and accept everyone, although they may go to a nonsmoker first, as they are sensitive to smells. This is why in the early stages only one person should speak to the pet. The rabbit will then associate the sound of that family member's voice with the scent of the individual.

Never/Always Advice

Even after rabbitproofing is complete, before your bunny's first release into your home environment, you should consider these guidelines.

Never. . .

- ever, chase your rabbit or you will end up doing it constantly. This may suit some people who never sit down, but it's not for everyone.
- let anyone give your pet conflicting orders. You do not need a rabbit with a split personality.
- let anyone tease, frighten, or confuse your rabbit. This is bound to happen from time to time, but try to avoid it in the early stages of training.
- use food rewards *at all.* There are a few minor exceptions suggested in this book, but it goes against the principle of voice training. This is the hardest thing the designated trainer has to get across to other family members.
- try to pick up and pet the bunny during the early stages of training. Later on your bunny will come to you willingly for petting—in fact, it will insist on being petted to the point of being a pest about it.

Always. . .

- be down at floor level to let your pet approach you.
- expect rabbits to stake out their territory by urinating and note what area they designate as their turf.
- expect to have to clean up urine and droppings in the early stages before housebreaking is complete.

This is not as alarming as it sounds.

- touch rabbits in the beginning *only* when they indicate they will tolerate it.
- give them ample time to scent you and know your voice.
- keep to a regular daily schedule for feeding, outings, and training.
- use their names in a warm tone of voice.
- have as many family members present as possible for their early outings.

Family Support Guidelines

- Only the trainer should discipline the rabbit.
- Only the trainer should handle the rabbit in a situation of stress.
- All parties in contact with the rabbit must consistently use the training commands previously decided upon and introduce no others.
- No person in the family other than the trainer may feed the rabbit greens or supplementary diet items as food rewards.
- No family member should ever give the rabbit table food of any kind (including cereals).
- No one should change the feeding and training routines except the trainer.
- All family members should clean the cage and feed the rabbit on a rotation basis at the same times of day.

Your Bunny's Debut

This is where the phrase "dumb bunny" can take on a whole new meaning. By the time you have created a "user-friendly bunny" you will have threatened the poor thing with becoming rabbit stew and four lucky-charm key chains for your friends. We took the advice contained in everything we read and this was our interpretation:

1. Put bunny on a table.
2. Pet and talk to bunny in soft tones.
3. Gently put bunny back in cage.
4. Repeat process daily until bunny is comfortable.

It didn't work like that! Either we had a bunny with a death wish or these instructions just did not apply to our Woodstock. Even with two of us standing at either side of a high circular glass table with arms linked around him, he wanted to take a flying leap. We were afraid that we might have adopted a bunny with suicidal tendencies. You may want to try the recommended method, as it does make sense, but if you run into the same scenario we experienced, you may want to consider an alternative method.

1. Have all family members present.
2. Enclose the space your rabbit will be permitted to move around in—i.e., close off all other rooms.

Getting to know your bunny means spending time at its level.

3. Have everyone on the floor at your pet's level encircling his allowed space. Preferably everyone should be sitting crosslegged or lying stomach down with arms outstretched, and close to the next family member. Lying flat on your stomach is preferable because it makes your height much less intimidating to your bunny.
4. Let your bunny explore each of you at random. There is no competition for affection involved. Bunnies are naturally curious and will sniff out everyone in the family in their own way in their own good time.
5. Whenever your bunny approaches a family member, that individual should slowly place a hand just in front of its nose at floor level without making contact.
6. If your bunny remains in front of your hand, you might try tentatively stroking it—but cease at the first sign of withdrawal. And never stroke your pet's fur in the wrong direction during the early stages.
7. When an individual family member is approached by the bunny, that person should be the only one to talk to it while it is scenting his or her hand. Bunnies rapidly learn to associate sound and smell. Nothing should interfere with this process, so televisions and stereos should be turned off.
8. Repeat these outings daily, with all family members in the same places at the same time, until your bunny accepts petting from everyone and does not evidence any real fright. At this point your pet is familiar with everyone's scent.
9. At the end of each session, a different family member should put the bunny back in its cage. This should be the same person who took the bunny out of its cage at the beginning of the session. By this method your pet will accept handling by the whole family.
10. Be certain that everyone understands that rabbits freeze or "play possum" when frightened; it's one of their natural defense mechanisms. Going into a freeze when touched does not necessarily indicate that it accepts petting.

Woodstock ceased his suicide mission under this plan. When we first saw the freeze posture we misunderstood it until we noticed that we could see white in the inside corners of his eyes. Then we realized that it was a sign of fright. He now goes into an immediate crouch when anyone puts a hand on his head, but unless I see white in his eyes I know he is hunkering down for a good petting session or a backscratch. It took only a few days of these sessions for him to accept us. I believe this was because there was no forced handling or petting.

Chapter 6
Handling Your Bunny

Recommended Handling

The first few times you handle your bunny can be frightening—at least they were for us. The proper way of picking up your rabbit initially is the same way you would pick up a kitten, or a small puppy—by the scruff of the neck over the shoulder blades and between the ears. *Never, ever* pick up a rabbit by its ears. This is a popular misconception about rabbits and is very cruel and painful to them.

1. Bend over and grip the loose skin at the scruff of the neck between the ears firmly in your fist, not between your fingers.
2. Lift the rabbit while rising to an upright position.
3. As quickly as possible, cradle its rump with your other hand in the recommended position.

The recommended position is to have the rabbit's rump in the palm of your hand and its head at the crook of your elbow. This position, however, gives you no control over your rabbit's forepaws, and unfortunately, didn't seem to do much for Wood-stock. The amount of first-aid cream I used to tend my many scratches told me there had to be another way to hold this weird bunny.

Most rabbits actually prefer to be held in a horizontal position. At first, I found that Woodstock wasn't too rambunctious in a vertical position with a hand supporting his rump and forepaws just below my shoulder, but that didn't last long. As he had my body to push against, he would cause me anxiety by trying to take a flying leap over my shoulder. A leap from this height could cause serious internal injury to a baby bunny. With something to push against, the strength of a rabbit's hind quarters is awesome.

Until Woodstock and I came to a better agreement, I found that the best way to hold him was to give him nothing to push against. To accomplish this, I would pick him up by the scruff of the neck with my right hand, and cradle his rump with my left on the way up. Then I would shift my right hand under his two front paws so that his left front leg was between my index and third fingers and his right front leg was hooked over my thumb. Simultaneously, I would turn

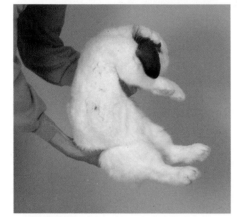

The recommended hold: Grasp your pet by the scruff of the neck.

Lift it carefully and immediately support its weight by placing your other hand under its rump.

Stand upright, holding the rump in the palm of one hand. The rabbit's head should rest at the crook of your elbow.

him so that his back was toward me and pull him close against my body. This meant all four paws were facing out. I saved myself a lot of embarrassment this way. All those scratches and scars were starting to become subjects of gossip!

The Woodstock Alternative Hold

Eventually we compromised on the recommended horizontal position, only in reverse. I placed his rump in the crook of my right arm and his forelegs in my right hand between my fingers and thumbs giving me control over his front legs. A plus to this method is that it allows you a free hand to stroke or tighten your hold if your pet should panic for any reason.

The most important thing to remember in handling your bunny in the early stages of training is to give your pet a sense of security in your arms. All household members should use the same hold in handling the rabbit and alway be conscious of the fact that a leap from a height could seriously injure your pet.

Be firm, but don't squeeze too tightly if the bunny squirms. If it seems really panic-stricken, quickly bend over and release it at knee level and try again later. Don't do what I did and try not to become intimidated by its strength—which is amazing—to say nothing of its speed as described in Chapter 9, Trust Training.

Expect some agitated behavior on the way down to ground level after

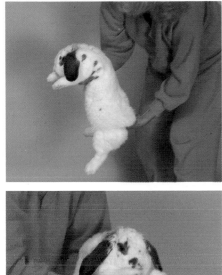

Left: Grasp your pet under the forelegs.
Right: Lift the rabbit, supporting it with a hand placed under its rump.

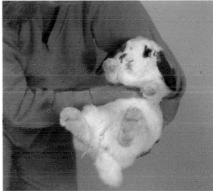

Left: Stand upright, move the rump toward the crook of your elbow.
Right: Keep the forelegs under control with your other hand.

you have been holding and petting your rabbit. Keep in mind that rabbits are born with the same two natural fears as humans: the fear of loud noises and the fear of falling. If you lose sight of your rabbit's natural fear of falling, you can expect to chalk up a few scratches while setting your pet down. The best way to proceed is to walk toward the cage, know exactly where the door is, and be sure that it is open. Do not bend over. Bend quickly from the knees, aim your pet at the door, and let go!

Now that Woodstock is a mature rabbit, I usually cart him around in one arm in an upside-down position, which he seems to have no objection to. When I want to release him, I just turn him away from me, bend over, and plop him into his cage.

Since Woodstock will freeze when anyone puts their hand on his head because he is anticipating a petting, we now pick him up under his forelegs. This is quite safe, and Woodstock just lies there waiting for something to happen. Never let anyone pick your rabbit up by its midsection or, if it tries to escape, by the hind quarters.

Other handling methods are explained in later chapters as they deal with different issues.

Chapter 7

Housekeeping and Grooming

This training is invaluable because it occurs early in your relationship and sets the stage for more advanced training. And secondly, it is the foundation for trust-training because it involves the most proprietary issue of the bunny world: its home.

Housekeeping

I began cleaning Woodstock's "commode" at floor level, and noticed that he would jump into his training tray while I was trying to empty it. To establish order, I would simply pick him up and gently move him aside, putting him close to the newspapers I use to line the pull-out tray under the wire-bottomed cage. He would always dig at the papers. I did not discipline him for this, since he so obviously enjoyed it and it allowed me time to wash, dry, and disinfect his large tray. After a few rounds of this routine, he went a little strange and started throwing the training tray around.

When you clean your rabbit's cage at floor level you are in close touch with your pet because you are in its comfort zone. Your bunny learns that this activity means its waste will be removed and is not alarmed. This also ensures that your bunny will not overreact in the future when its home is being invaded.

At about six months of age, Woodstock wasn't disturbed when I put the large tray on the counter for cleaning, but I was nervous at first when he would circle my feet while I was trying to clean the tray. However when I put the small training tray on the floor where he could play with it, he seemed much calmer. This made cleanup times less strenuous and I didn't have to keep picking him up and moving him. Also, I had a lot less shredded newspaper.

If your bunny becomes agitated during the cleaning process, immediately put the tray on the floor and let your pet jump into it. Talk to your bunny until it settles down. You can then gently lift it out and continue to clean the tray at floor level.

I discovered that housekeeping chores were best done just before Woodstock's evening feeding because he was exercised and would be calm, smelling his dinner in a clean cage. He normally flops after eating.

During the housebreaking stage, the less your bunny has in its system, the less it has to void when it becomes excited as you clean the cage.

Grooming

In the beginning I didn't realize that just picking Woodstock up during the shedding seasons meant a fur coat on my clothing. I couldn't believe he could shed so much fur simply on contact. However, if you start the grooming process fairly quickly you will find that you can survive the shedding seasons without concern. First introduce your rabbit to a wire or bristle brush. If you leave the brush on the floor during your pet's outing it will adopt it as a possession by chinning it. We started Woodstock in the right direction by putting the brush in his cage.

Be at floor level, and when your bunny approaches you, have the brush handy and attempt to stroke the rabbit with it. Do not force this gesture; your pet will respond in time. Woodstock now flops and waits for either a back rub or a good brushing.

Housekeeping performed at ground level will seem less threatening to your pet.

Soiled newspapers can be folded and disposed of quickly and easily.

Be prepared for a visit from Inspector Rabbit.

Obviously a job well done!

Chapter 8
Rabbitry: Reading Body Language

Unlike most other domestic pets, rabbits have no way of communicating with their family by vocal sounds. They can, however, make low audible sounds that you can pick up if you are close enough. They tend to communicate the only way they know how—through body language. Learning their body language is important. Even senior executives of major corporations spend considerable money in training to understand human body language to improve their negotiating skills. Close observation of Woodstock was an eye-opener in bunny body language.

Bunnies can be comical and quite surprising to your guests. When Woodstock plays Mario Andretti around our living room, he leaves our guests speechless. He can leap small coffee tables in a single bound. Since he doesn't discriminate, he'll approach anyone without encouragement. All we need do is interpret for him to our guests. (See Voice Training in Chapter 9.) Here is what we discovered:

Racing Around

Woodstock uses his permitted space like a racetrack as soon as he's been given his freedom. I have to expect that the first ten minutes will be used by him to make sure that his territory has not been invaded by another bunny when he wasn't looking. He will "chin" everything he considers his, including me! He will also investigate anything new. This includes bags of groceries, briefcases, guests, and pretty well anything left lying around at ground level. He will also "chin" anything new to mark it as exclusively his. He will show curiosity toward new objects or people by standing up on his hind legs to get a better perspective and then stake out the object of his investigation by "chinning" it.

Chinning

This practice seems to be more predominant in the buck (male) than in the doe (female). Rabbits have a scent gland under their chins; the secretions from this gland are only discernable to other rabbits. They rub this gland on anything they wish to identify as theirs. This includes people. In the wild, this identifies territorial boundaries to other rabbits. Woodstock used to rub his chin on my nose while I was lying on the floor with him. He still nudges or chins our feet when he first comes out of his cage. Perhaps this is to remind us that we still belong to him.

The secretion is totally odorless and feels only slightly damp. He sometimes follows this with licks, a sign of strong affection. I have to wonder about this, however, when he licks the sofa. Anything bunnies feel proprietary about is fair game, including your guests. Shoes, handbags, briefcases, elbows, hands, feet, ankles, and legs are all up for chinning. They won't approach or chin anyone they feel threatened by. Woodstock's reactions to acquaintances and people provide a new type of barometer, and I tend to give his reactions to strangers at least some credence.

Circling

From everything I read "before Woodstock," this is supposed to indicate ownership, but my experience is that it can also indicate trouble! You haven't lived until you've had a bunny bite on the rump. The greater the speed, the more danger you may be in. When faced by a rapidly circling rabbit, it is wise to stop what you are doing and give it some affection.

Circling Positives

Your rabbit circles you and continues to close the diameter of the circle. If you are sitting with another family member, your pet may run figure eights around both of you. Woodstock does this with different people, which means that he accepts both individuals equally. He can make anyone dizzy with the number of circles he makes—and then he changes direction and circles the other way.

I can't say I understand what this means except that maybe he makes himself dizzy and has to change direction. We did notice that he takes about the same number of turns in each direction.

Circling Negatives

This one I learned the hard way, not with Woodstock, but with Smokey, a friend's rabbit. Smokey, like all bunnies, was very proprietary about his cage and his girlfriend, Benji. While I was cleaning their cages so our friends could sleep in on a Saturday morning of a weekend visit, Smokey began wildly circling me. I kept gently pushing him out of the way. He must have become frustrated enough to decide to indulge himself with a bite of rump roast! The nip is rarely harmful, but be aware that if you are cleaning a cage and the bunny starts wildly circling you, you may be subject to a nip at whatever part of your anatomy happens to be in sight. If children are to be responsible for cage-cleaning duty, you should tell them about the rabbit's possessive nature. Humans appreciate housekeeping service, but bunnies don't seem to mind living without it.

Digging and Crouching

With Woodstock this turned out to be a sign that he would urinate. Other books told me that digging is a sign that the rabbit wants affection, but for Stocky it was a sure sign that urination would follow. In the early stages of our relationship and before we had him neutered, he would dig at my clothes. This can hurt because of a rabbit's strength and the sharpness of its claws, even when they have been clipped. Breaking him of this habit was done by voice training—a "No-no-no" command. If I give Woodstock attention when he is digging, he may react in one of two ways. Either positively, by flattening out for a good petting, or negatively, pushing my hand away with his nose. You must understand that bunnies have individual personalities and, like people, they have their moods.

Periscoping

Rabbits will raise themselves on their hind legs to get a better view and may remain in this posture for over a minute. This means that your pet is very curious about something. I have seen Woodstock in this posture for over two minutes in front of a wall, but I couldn't tell you what was so interesting to him.

Right: Rabbits in the wild periscope frequently to watch for predators.

Teeth Grinding and Low Growling

Woodstock will grind his teeth while being held and petted, and by his breathing and the look on his masked-bandit face I know that this is a definite sign of pure bliss. I have read that low growling is a similar indication and while I have not experienced it with Stocky, some of my friends tell me they have heard it.

Other interpretations of bunny body language are explained in Chapter 9, Trust Training, and Close Encounters of the Fourth Kind in Chapter 10.

Chapter 9
Trust-Training

Bunny Air-O-Bics

Trust-training begins when you first bring your bunny home and requires patience and understanding. First of all, your bunny should feel perfectly secure within its territory. Whether or not it does will be revealed by its active behavior outside of the cage. Woodstock lets us know how he feels by his antics, which we have dubbed "Bunny Air-O-Bics." These include:

- **Rainbow leaps** in the living room, sometimes with high arcs over low tables.

- **Half gainers,** which are horizontal leaps at high speeds while twisting the rump.

- **Helicopter leaps,** which consist of jumps straight up with a 190-degree turn in the air. Upon landing, Woodstock looks around as if puzzled that he is not facing the same direction he took off in.

- **Sidewinders** are low jumps straight up and sideways, both at the same time. This is usually followed by the racing superstar.

- **Racing superstar** is a high-speed run with occasional crashes into walls, refrigerator, stove, dishwasher, and other furniture. This is

Left: You can call your rabbit home by strumming on the wires of its cage.
Right: Don't slam the cage door immediately, so your pet won't associate the command with punishment.

sometimes accompanied by missing the door to his cage and nearly knocking himself senseless.

- **Speed burrows** is a dive-and-run combination behind furniture with a speedy backup. Apparently bunnies can move as fast in reverse as in forward. I wish I could do as well in my car.
- **El floppo** consists of sudden flops on his side against walls or furniture. As Woodstock is a minilop, on the run the ears of this racing superstar stand out like airplane propellers and when he flops, one usually flips back and up.
- **El stretcho** is a different version of El floppo. Woodstock stretches out on his stomach with back legs out as far as they can go, or on his side with front and back paws crossed. This usually follows a particularly strenuous Air-O-Bics session.

Once you have gauged his mood by his antics, you can begin the training session. I never attempted training until Woodstock had worked off some steam. Regardless of your bunny's behavior, I would suggest that you give your pet at least a 15-minute outing before you begin so that it starts out feeling a freedom of movement.

Voice Training

Believe it or not, you can control your rabbit by voice training. The first rule is to *Never, ever* raise your voice to your pet except in an emergency.

If you voice-train your pet correctly, you should never have to chase or physically discipline it. I haven't had to correct Woodstock in this manner. Most domestic pets are disciplined by a tap on the nose. This is totally inappropriate for rabbits. They are very sensitive and require little discipline if properly trained with affection and, above all, patience.

During Woodstock's housebreaking period, it was only when he urinated to stake out his territory that I would discipline him by any other method than by voice tone. I would hold him at the place of the accident firmly but gently and say "No, no, no, Woodstock." Then I would scoop him up and, repeating the phrase in gentle tones while walking him to his cage, put him inside and close the cage door.

It took less than three weeks to completely housebreak him using this method.

Rules of Voice Training

1. Know what you want your pet to become.
2. Be realistic—understand rabbitry.
3. Use simple one-word commands.
4. Be self-disciplined; do not train only sporadically.
5. Set your own disciplines before you set your rabbit's.
6. Establish what reward system you will be using.
7. Have patience. User-friendly bunnies are not created overnight.

Command	Translation
Home, Woodstock!	Go to your cage, you rotten rabbit!
No,No,No,No,No, Woodstock!	If you don't stop doing that you'll be rabbit stew tonight!
Up Woodstock!	Jump into my lap, you cute little thing!
Come on, Woodstock!	Come here! Don't confuse "Come on" with "Up!" This command is necessary for outdoor training.
It's O.K., Woodstock.	There's nothing to be afraid of, you dumb bunny!
Treats, Woodstock.	Exactly what it says. Don't use this phrase unless you have one or you may be risking your life.
Thump*	Danger. He'll freeze when he hears this and you can easily pick him up or retrieve him.

*Thump is a vocal command accompanied by stamping your foot.

Applying the Rules

Decide on a list of simple one-word commands based on what can reasonably be expected from a rabbit. *Always* use your pet's name after every command word. The list of commands above is Woodstock's dictionary at the present time.

Training the Commands

The commands listed are in order of training, although several commands were presented simultaneously without confusing Woodstock.

Thump, Woodstock was the first command initiated. I had read in rabbit books that rabbits "thump" or "tap" with a hind leg to transmit danger signals to their fellow rabbits. It occurred to me early in our relationship that if I didn't want to chase Woodstock constantly when he was up to some mischief, perhaps I could use this natural rabbit trait combined with some psychology. In the experimental stage, whenever I saw him misbehaving I would stamp my foot on the floor. He seemed to react as if another rabbit was signaling danger and would immediately freeze. This saved many miles on my Addidas. It then occurred to me to add a vocal command. Because of our carpeting, this activity sounded like a thump to him, so I adopted the word "thump" to reinforce this action. I was quite amazed at the result of what was just a good idea at the time. The closer you can imitate your rabbit's thump or tap, the more effective the results. In outdoor training you must really stamp your foot hard so that your rabbit hears it clearly.

In using the "Thump, Woodstock"

Woodstock still has a taste for telephone wires...

command, I discovered that all this would accomplish was to stop him from doing whatever mischief he was up to. Since it breaks their attention span, rabbits will usually tear off to other rabbity activities, which means they may immediately find other forms of entertainment at your expense.

Home, Woodstock is, without a doubt, the most valuable command you can use. But understand that it takes a few weeks to train and a lot of patience. The reason why Woodstock responded as quickly as he did is because the command was constantly reinforced by others as well.

Woodstock still thwarts me once in a while, but now that he is mature and has maximum freedom, we rarely need to coax him home. From the very first excursion out, when you want your bunny back in its cage, sit on the floor next to the cage but do not block the entrance. If you run your fingertips over the cage or tap on the food or water container you will get your rabbit's attention by the sound. Since the position of the cage is instantly known by smell and location, your bunny is bound to be curious. Remember that rabbits have notoriously poor eyesight and respond to sounds and scents. Your bunny

...but a simple "No, no, no, no, Woodstock" will stop him almost immediately.

will scent both his cage and your proximity to it, and the sounds you make on his cage will act almost like a homing device.

However, beware! After a short time Woodstock realized that when he went home on command his door would be shut on him. I didn't want him to associate the command with punishment, consequently, the next step was to leave the door open while sitting beside it so he could leap back out. For a while he played Jack-in-the-Box. I accelerated the process by putting greens in his cage while he was on an outing, leaving the door open, and giving the "Home, Wood-

stock!" command. He now knows that if the cage door is closed after he goes home it is neither reward nor punishment. Punishment to Woodstock is when I physically retrieve him, put him inside, and close the door. Whenever that is necessary, he sulks, followed by an "El floppo" and a nap.

No, No, No, No, Woodstock! This command takes the most badgering and the most consistent reinforcement but it's worth every effort. The words are run together—i.e., "No-no-no-no, Woodstock!" Every time you give the command when your rabbit is up to something dangerous or mischievous, if your pet does not cease immediately, you must scoop it up, carry it to the cage—repeating softly "No-no-no-no"—close the door, and leave it alone. This is where the dumb bunny gets smart—it doesn't take very long for the message to sink in. I don't think I could live without this command—I can discipline Woodstock from across the room while watching TV! According to the rabbit owners I've researched, bunny retention is quite high. Once they've got it, it stays. Obviously, patience is the key and voice intonation, the lock.

Up, Woodstock! When Woodstock was about 20 weeks old, I was getting tired of being on the floor all the time with my rabbit. Finally it occurred to me to train a command that would bring him to me, instead of the other way around. I tried calling to him and when he would come over to where I was sitting, I would pat the chair or sofa beside me, or my lap, and say "Up, Woodstock!" Total disinterest! It was frustrating when he would run right over as paged and then sit there looking at me. When I'd reach down to pick him up to show him what I expected, while repeating "Up, Woodstock!" off he'd go before I could get my hands on him. I was deflated, considering we had done so well with previous commands. There had to be another way to accomplish this.

This is the only other departure I took from voice training. Out of desperation, I opted for food rewards.

Voila! I waved a small piece of carrot in front of his nose, leaned back, and said "Up, Woodstock!" and there he was. I gave him the food reward, and did not attempt to restrain him afterward. Within three days, he would leap up on command.

Each day the food reward became smaller and by day three he was sniffing around for what simply was no longer there. Today, if anyone visits and overemphasizes the word "up," they will get a bunny in their lap. Unfortunately, it did not occur to me at the time to teach a "Down, Woodstock!" command.

With the "Up, Woodstock" command I found I had a bunny on my hands who had discovered the joys of leaping on furniture and exploring interesting things *above* floor level. This experience must have opened a whole new vista of potential mischief for him. He explored every table, desk, chair, and sofa in our home. (He almost learned his lesson when he leaped into the bathtub but discovered it was too slippery for him to leap out!)

Come on, Woodstock! This command is invaluable in outdoor training. It indicates to your rabbit that you want it to come to you immediately. I first trained Woodstock outdoors with this command on a harness and a lead. I put him on a 15-foot (5m) lead, walked away from him, turned and called "Come on, Woodstock!" When he didn't respond, I gave him a very gentle tug on the lead. It takes patience, but your rabbit will respond if it is used to responding to indoor commands. I use this command indoors when I want Woodstock to follow me. (For more details, see Chapter 11, Outdoor Training.)

It's O.K., Woodstock! This is not so much a command as a comforting statement. It calms your pet after you have scooped it up in your arms and are stroking or trancing. (See Chapter 11 for "trancing") Woodstock recognizes these words when he is under stress because they are never used at any other time. To teach the command, you must constantly say it in soft tones while holding and stroking your bunny.

Treats, Woodstock! I use this command sparingly. We have a "killer" cockatiel named Tweetie and by accident I found that rabbits feel about birdseed the way kids feel about ice cream. Tweetie resides on the top shelf of a stand—the penthouse—and Woodstock has the basement apartment—his cage is housed in the lower portion of the stand. Tweetie tends to throw her seeds around indiscriminately and, inevitably, some land on the shelf outside the cage and some end up in Woodstock's cage. When Woodstock took a flying three-foot leap up to Tweetie's stand after her birdseed, we realized this was "treats" to him. Seeds are like candy to bunnies and, fed sparingly, not harmful.

If you are going to give treats once in a while, there should be a vocal command to indicate your action. When all else fails and you say the word "treats," you will have instant bunny company. Be sure you have the treat in your hand before you even think about uttering the word.

Down, Woodstock! Rabbits tend to explore at the ground level. User-friendly bunnies, however, will be curious about most anything and will take rainbow leaps onto furniture. We reserved the one sofa out of three that we use for watching TV so that he would know the difference between what he was permitted to leap on and what he wasn't. The "No-no-no-no, Woodstock" command kept him from the other two sofas, and the "Up, Woodstock" command brought him to us. To train the "down" command, I would stand over him, snap my fingers, point downward and say "Down, Woodstock!" If he didn't respond quickly, I would scoop him up and put him in his cage, whereupon he would sulk and go El floppo.

I'm sure there are many other commands rabbit owners can train but the most important thing to consider is to be realistic in your expectations.

If we need to leave Woodstock in anyone's care, I give them a card with the commands and what they mean to him. It is advisable to provide written documentation about your pet's dietary habits, times of day for feeding, exercise times, and your veterinarian's emergency number. Never permit anyone bunnysitting your pet to feed it anything that you have not provided or to feed your bunny on a different schedule from that of its home environment.

Left: Woodstock checks out my sofa...
Right: ...turns his back when I gently scold him.

Left: ...seems determined to ignore me...
Right: ...but finally responds to a stern, "Down Woodstock."

Chapter 10
Losing the Fear of the Explosive Bunny!

Peter, our breeder, told us that minilops are generally bred for their docility. Woodstock must have been an exception. We wondered if there was possibly some kind of "upper" in our municipal water system. When he decides to explode, you'd have to have as many arms as an octopus to contain him—it is truly an awesome sight, complete with fur tufts flying! You can't help but think some clever person should have invented a straitjacket for this preferred pet of the future.

Woodstock's size, strength, and my nervousness about handling him made my early handling experiences frightening. And I'm sure that most animals sense these feelings in humans. Also, I didn't want to squeeze him too tightly. Because of all this, it probably took him a little longer than most to recognize who was the boss. Some days I'm still not sure. Bunnies are nocturnal and I still find his evening outings hard to handle.

Sooner or later you will have to come to grips with your pet, and I

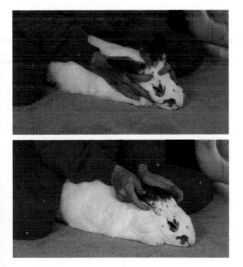

Left: Most rabbits love to have their cheeks massaged. Right: Woodstock also enjoys having his ears gently pulled.

Left: After a few minutes... Right: ... Woodstock enters a state of deep relaxation.

45

mean this literally. In the beginning I forced myself to pick Woodstock up at different times during his outings to see how he would react. He would be docile while he was in my arms or in my lap being petted, but suddenly he would go into a mad scramble. This always took me by surprise and I never knew where the claw marks were going to show up the next day. Consequently, I took to wearing long-sleeved blouses or jackets.

If you own any of the dwarf breeds you will not have to be as concerned because they are not as strong. They are, however, known to be hyperactive. Woodstock, at this point, was the size of a large house cat or a small dog and definitely in the "I'm in command" mode. I'm at a loss to explain why I didn't have his claws clipped at this time. I certainly recommend it when the rabbit is six months old. I'm sure it can be done sooner but I wanted my rabbit to have full traction and the opportunity to know his own strength. Also, I don't believe in altering nature without a good reason. Obviously, I found good reason later with the physical evidence of Woodstock's exuberance!

Trancing

The fastest way to lose your fear of the explosive bunny is to learn how to *trance* it. When held in the right position, rabbits will go into a trance. I only wish I had known about this phenomenon earlier in our relationship. However, while totally ignorant of this interesting trait, I accidentally put a friend's bunny into a trance. At the time I knew little about rabbits and didn't feel this was anything unusual. I just thought I had a cute bunny on my hands. My friend's astonishment didn't register either. Now that I know the benefits of trancing, I highly recommend the process whenever your bunny becomes hyperactive. It is particularly valuable if your rabbit has been threatened by a predator outdoors and has just been rescued by you. It can have an almost instant calming effect.

The Process

To accomplish this little trick of rabbit psychology, hold the rabbit close to your body and upside down so that it is resting on its back with its rump supported and all four paws sticking out in the air. Depending upon whether you are right- or lefthanded, keep the predominant hand under the forelegs to hold your pet. Stroke its head from the tip of its nose past its ears, making sure the cheeks are stroked in the process. You will be able to gauge the state of trance by your pet's breathing and visible relaxation. If you are sitting with the rabbit in your lap, you should be able to remove the confining hand and use both hands to stroke its cheeks. Don't be alarmed if you see the hind paws quiver. This goes with trancing and tells you that your bunny is deeply into it. Rabbits may stretch out in your lap in total bliss if they go deep enough. My friend's rabbit did—but not Woodstock!

My Woodstock will trance, but be aware that rabbits can come out of a trance as fast as they go into it. Be prepared for anything, such as a sudden flying leap or a mad scramble, even up or over your shoulder. Rabbits lying on their backs can flip over amazingly fast if they are not held down, which I do not recommend in trust-training. Do not attempt to confine your rabbit when it is coming out of a trance. Permit your pet to take off at will and, believe me, it will!

The Fear Syndrome

Eventually, you will have to face the fact that you are bigger, stronger, and smarter than your bunny, and assert yourself in the way you handle your pet. It takes time because gentleness during the bunny's infancy (6 to 15 weeks) pays the most dividends in trust-training. It is far better to fear hurting your pet in the way you and others handle it than to be too aggressive. You certainly don't need a traumatized rabbit.

As your pet matures, you will find it much easier to handle, and it should only show resistance when in an obstinate mood. Bunnies do indeed have moods. Woodstock can be quite obstreperous if he wants a backscratch and doesn't get it upon nudging.

The best way to overcome your handling fears is to understand that rabbits are timid by nature; when you see signs of the "explosive bunny" it is because your pet is comfortable and feels enough at home in its environment to assert its own needs.

Take note of your rabbit's traits. For example:

- What time of day is it most/least affectionate?
- Where does it prefer communicating? (At floor level; on the sofa; etc.)
- To whom does it relate best? At what times? Under what circumstances?
- Whom does it follow around?

Armed with this knowledge, you can assert yourself as the trainer. Early in the training period, use gentleness and warm tones to guide your pet into a trusting relationship. Whenever I was frustrated with Woodstock, I would think "Hop a mile in my paws!" Most of the time it enabled me to treat him with the love and care he deserved. Don't let anyone overreact to the explosive bunny. As I've said before, rabbits will always do rabbity things.

Close Encounters of the Fourth Kind

Despite their docile nature, rabbits resist dominance in four distinct ways: nonchalance, stubbornness, wild activity, and bids for attention. Even a family quarrel can disturb your pet and provoke these behavioral traits. Bucks may also exhibit aggressive behavior when in a mating

Trancing can be used effectively...

mood. Before Woodstock was neutered, he would madly circle me and pull on my pants or jeans or, if I was wearing shorts, lick my calf and, if ignored, give me a nip.

Nonchalance

This can be an exhibition of face- and ear-grooming immediately following a command, or back turning, or any other bunny body language that indicates you are being totally ignored.

Stubbornness

This posture is manifested as rebelliousness as your bunny will immediately do something it has been trained specifically not to do.

Wild Activity

This may mean a hide-and-seek game plan designed to surprise you with a whole new road map of hard-to-be-retrieved-from spots your bunny discovered and has been keeping in reserve for the occasion.

...whenever and wherever your rabbit becomes overly excited.

Attention Bid

Under extreme duress your pet will use the only form of communication left. It is advisable to consider the cause of aggravation if your pet, after it is housebroken, suddenly presents you with droppings.

Coping with Encounters of the Fourth Kind

Nonchalance

This calls for the same behavior from you. Just talk your bunny down or ignore it. Do not show signs of agitation. When Woodstock senses that his face-grooming or other signals are having no affect, he will respond to the original command. Do not leave your pet; it will eventually respond. If Woodstock does not react within three minutes, I pick him up

and put him in his cage and by voice tone (never loud) let him know he has been "bad."

Stubbornness

Woodstock ranges from ornary early in the evening to downright destructive as the hour gets later. Rabbits are nocturnal. My advice is to accept this behavior as rabbity and not to overreact to it. If the "No-no-no-no" command does not achieve the desired result, a little communication from you at ground level should do the trick. Stocky demands most of his affection at night and will go to any lengths to achieve his goal.

Wild Activity

Mad circling and digging at your clothes are examples of agitation. Chances are that your rabbit wants some affection but probably does not want to be picked up. Petting without confinement should satisfy your bunny's need. When petted Woodstock will sit still for anywhere from thirty seconds to five minutes before dashing away to other rabbity endeavors.

Attention Bid

Some form of threat is involved. It may be a stranger in your home, a sudden loud noise, or a predatory visitor such as a dog or a cat that your pet scents. Understand that bunnies do not normally urinate or defecate after housebreaking unless under extreme stress. Discipline in this case is not recommended. Simply clean up the accident and analyze the cause so that you can attempt to avoid recurances.

When rabbits play hide and seek it can be very frustrating. Woodstock has a favorite spot under a rocking chair that I converted into a planter. No matter which angle I approach it from he has another way to exit. Once he's gone and I'm back on my feet, I have to look around for him. By the time I've found him, in a blur of speed he's back under the rocker again. This seems to give him a lot of satisfaction. I simply walk away and ignore him or, if in a hurry, tap on his food trough at his cage, which is a sure way to bring him hopping home.

Chapter 11
Outdoor Training

When your rabbit can be trusted to respond to your indoor training commands, you may want to introduce your pet to the great outdoors.

Woodstock was exposed to both a house and an apartment. Here is what I discovered about the two.

The House Bunny

If you have a house with a backyard, as long as it is properly fenced, you should be able to give your pet maximum freedom. In the early stages, use a harness with at least a 15-foot (2.74 m) lead. While your rabbit is exploring its newfound freedom, keep the lead around your wrist or in your hand and let your bunny walk you. I learned quickly that you do not walk a rabbit. It happens in reverse.

I could not leave my little rascal unattended or where I could not see him. In an urban backyard setting, Woodstock would panic at the noises of large vehicles like buses or trucks, which have a strong effect on his auditory senses. When that happened, he would go into a mad run-and-dive state that would take him into nearby bushes from which he'd have to be coaxed out. In the process, he would tangle his lead in the shrubbery. One of the interesting things I discovered was that outdoors Woodstock was capable of short sprints at high speeds but would not attempt to venture any further. If, while in his "cover zone" under the bushes, he was again frightened, he tended just to play possum rather than to head for uncharted territory.

For the backyard bunny, it is important to understand that your primary concerns are:

A travel cage will give your pet a feeling of security during your outings.

- Proper fencing in your yard.
- No insecticides at your rabbit's level. To gauge this, you should consider your pet at full stretch. For example, when your rabbit rests on its haunches and stretches up to look around, you will know at what height you need to provide protection from insecticides. You can never be too cautious.
- A lookout for predators. In a rural or urban setting, dogs, cats, squirrels, and even airborn predators such as hawks are your rabbit's natural enemies.
- A lookout for people who may see your rabbit and want to visit without permission.
- A watch on your garden, if you have one, particularly an herb garden. You do not need a sick rabbit on your hands because it dove into your backyard garden as though it were a bunny candy store.

Homeowners have an advantage in that, with a little chicken wire, a rabbit run can be created, which means less supervision outdoors. It does *not,* however, mean no supervision.

Much of the information under "Apartment Bunny" will apply to the homeowner as well.

The Apartment Bunny

Preparing for Your Rabbit's Outings

Woodstock taught me some invaluable clues to rabbit mentality for planning an outing. Do not expect to pick your bunny up, clip it to a lead, and say "Let's go!" It just doesn't work that way!

Woodstock responded best when I gave him at least five to ten minutes to do his normal rabbity routine around the apartment. He needed to assure himself that no other rabbit had invaded his territory, to chin all of "his things," and to be comfortable within his domain.

This is a two-way street. While he was doing this, I had the opportunity to make sure I had everything organized for his outing. My checklist is:

- Harness and lead
- Travel cage
- A well-defined plan for the excursion
- A check on the weather forecast
- A carrot or other treat for emergencies
- A blanket to sit on, if park-bound

Use a long leash when strolling in the park.

- A full water bottle
- A good book or the company of a friend who's read one
- A camera
- Keys handy

Harnessing the Explosive Bunny

Lightweight nylon harnesses for cats are available in every pet store. Before shopping, measure your pet around the midsection as well as the neck, as there is two critical measurements—the neck size and the chest size. I didn't do this and it took three rounds before I achieved the right fit. I underestimated Woodstock's build—the same mistake I make with Peter. I thought I was buying for the svelte bunny when I should have been buying for the stocky bunny. Hence, Woodstock's nickname has always been "Stocky" to me and "Woody" to Peter.

In the beginning, Peter would hold Woodstock while I put his harness on him. Then it occurred to me that Petey might not always be around when I wanted to take Woodstock on an outing and I would have to harness my explosive bunny on my own. Here is what works:

Use a kitchen counter or a high table that has a smooth, unscratchable surface. I put Stocky on the kitchen counter, put my hand on his head, and stroke his cheeks. This causes him to go into an immediate freeze-and-crouch position. From there on it's a downhill run.

It is easy to put on the harness. I avoid any activity under his chin, as this is not his favorite sport. I turn the harness to the side so that I'm working next to his ear. Once this part is fastened, I again stroke his cheeks, head, and ears. I then find it easy to slide my hand under his midsection and fasten the chest strap, again on the side. Then I simply slide the entire harness around so that it is under him in the right position for fastening to the lead.

It is important that you avoid making the harness too tight. You should be able to fit the tip of your little finger under the harness at the neck position. It is equally important that you know your rabbit's strength and fasten the harness so that it fits snugly. A friend was panicstricken when her rabbit, frightened by a dog in a park, literally leaped out of its harness and took off. Obviously, she had fastened it too loosely that day, and after she scared off the predator and retrieved her rabbit, she never made that mistake again.

Apartment Elevators

Apartment dwellers should never lose sight of the fact that rabbits have a natural fear of heights, so the first time you take your rabbit on an elevator be prepared for it to react to the downward motion. This means that unless your pet is in a travel cage, you should have a firm grip because your rabbit may try to scramble. By this time, you will probably have observed this trait when bending over to release your bunny. Somehow, upward motion doesn't seem to have the same effect. Woodstock is now accustomed to the elevator and is also always held close and talked to. Never put your pet on the floor of an elevator unless it is in its travel cage. I found that using the stairs instead of the elevator was less stressful to Stocky.

You will have to juggle keys, your rabbit, and other objects while opening doors, talking to neighbors, and manipulating parcels. This is where the harness and lead come in handy. You can always put your bunny down if you keep the lead looped around your wrist. So that I don't trip over it, I stuff the slack into my pocket or purse on the same side as I am holding him.

Outdoor Routines

Your routine should be consistent in the experimental stage of outdoor excursions. Always take your pet to the same location. Constant vocal contact is the best control over your bunny outdoors. With a 15-foot (2.74 m) lead your pet should rarely tug on it; your pet should also be responsive to vocal commands coupled with its name. I found that Woodstock, when frightened, runs right back to my side and goes into a freeze. That is, if he has not dived into some nearby shrubbery.

Rabbits, unlike humans, are not sun worshippers. I found that when I wanted some sun the best compromise was to stretch out in the sun next to the shade of a tree with Woodstock's lead around my wrist. In the beginning, it is beneficial to be lying down at your rabbit's level. The great outdoors is rather frightening to a domestic rabbit and if your pet is frightened, this posture enables your pet to hear and see you better in order to find you quickly.

Later, you can sit up crosslegged and you will be delighted when you see your pet stand up on its hind legs to look around for you. When Woodstock tugs a lot on his lead it means he's sufficiently comfortable with his environment to be bored and wants to explore more territory. You should be considerate and stand up and permit him to "walk you."

Never try to lead your bunny if you want to keep its trust and affection. You will know how relaxed and content your pet is in the outdoors when, stretched out on its stomach, nibbling at grass, it looks as though it were stalking. Woodstock stretches his hind legs behind him and inches forward, still on his stomach.

Outdoor Health and Safety

Certain plants should be avoided, as well as grass that has been sprayed with insecticide. Take heart—the phrase "dumb bunny" doesn't seem to apply to most domestic rabbits when it comes to their

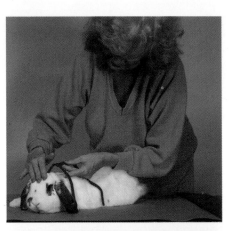

Always harness your rabbit from the side.

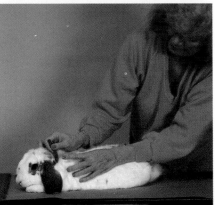

Fasten the neck strap first.

Pull the chest strap into place...

eating habits. Woodstock turns up his nose at day-old parsley or carrots which are perfectly palatable. You should, however, be able to identify harmful plants when you see them in a park or in the woods. An accurate list of hazardous plants can be found on page 23.

If you put your bunny down on concrete, such as a walkway, driveway, paved road, or sidewalk, be certain that the concrete is not at a temperature that you wouldn't step on yourself barefooted. Concrete helps keep your bunny's claws worn down. Remember that the minute you put your rabbit down it might be 10 to 15 feet (2.74 to 3.05 m) away from you, even on its lead, so be careful of traffic.

Safety Tips

When a dog, cat, or squirrel is within your range of vision, instantly retrieve your rabbit and, as stated earlier, be alert for large birds as well. Always be on the watch for anything that might frighten your pet. Chances are that your rabbit will sense danger before you do and will either run straight to you or try to bolt. If it bolts, you will feel a strong tug on the lead and should be prepared to react immediately. In the early stages of outdoor training you should not anchor your rabbit's lead to anything but your wrist so that you can feel any alarm instantly. Haul your rabbit in and scoop it up in your arms immediately. This is where the harness comes in handy, as you can lift your pet quickly by the harness without harming it in any way. Even when you have your rabbit in your arms, both of you may now be threatened by an aggressive dog or cat and your pet may react in terror with a mad scramble and an attempted suicide leap. You must keep a firm grip for protection. Avoid any confrontation with the predator.

It is best to turn your back on the threatening animal and walk swiftly away to where you can put your pet in your car or its travel cage. When outdoors, I always keep Stocky's travel cage close to me as it is almost impossible for an attacking animal to penetrate an enclosed cage. If you are able to rescue and put your pet in a travel cage before an attack, do not attempt to confront the predator. That way the worse that can happen is a slightly traumatized bunny.

Most domestic dogs and cats have been trained by their owners not to bite humans, but you should never show fear. Don't try to cope with the attacking animal; you'll have your hands full with your bunny. Do not put your rabbit down. Holding your pet, walk quickly to your car or home, keeping your back to the offending animal. You can always return to collect the cage. Since most animals are accompanied by their owners, when in doubt, holler for help.

The reason I strongly recommend a harness and lead at all times outdoors is that it helps if you need to rescue your rabbit. I simply shorten my grip on the lead hand over hand while talking to Stocky and make a

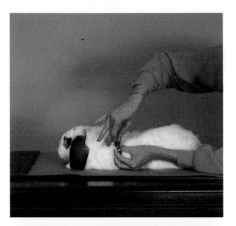

...fasten it, and slide the entire harness into position.

Check to make sure the straps are not too tight.

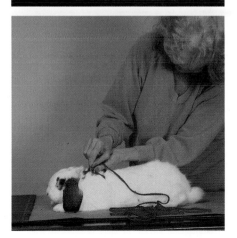

Attach the leash.

quick grab at the harness. If I see something that I know he has not yet sensed, I never jerk on the lead so that he isn't alarmed.

Other Hazards

Be prepared for children to approach your pet outdoors, as bunnies are practically irresistible to them. However, try to keep them from handling your pet until you give them a few basic instructions on approaching and managing your pet properly. I took Woodstock to a client's company barbecue to entertain the children and died a thousand deaths worrying about whether he might nip someone. He was the star of the show, but on the other hand, I caught the children in the nick of time about to put Stocky in the hot tub. It seems that trained rabbits don't feel unduly threatened by children.

Keep a constant vigil over your rabbit's outdoor environment for its safety. And never, ever let anyone babysit your pet outdoors, even for a short time. They would not have enough knowledge to be responsible for protecting your pet.

Chapter 12
Fixing Your Bunny

Signs That the Time Has Come

If you are living with a male rabbit (buck) that has reached sexual maturity, it may be about eight to ten months before the signs are obvious. He will become more agitated when he wants to mate. The advice given to me was to have Woodstock neutered when he was approximately one year old. This is about the same for the female (doe). Both sexes exhibit traits similar to other domestic animals.

Taking the advice of dedicated rabbit owners and breeders, I mentally scheduled Woodstock for an anatomical adjustment in February—he had been born in mid-January of the previous year. Somehow, business commitments intervened and he escaped his fate until late April. From February to April he was still cute but I realized I should not have procrastinated. Here are a few messages you may receive that will indicate your buck has reached maturity.

Your rabbit will probably focus on one family member as a surrogate mate, and he or she will be favored with any combination of the following bunny romancing gifts:

- Wild circling and love bites. These are never vicious but are often surprising.
- Spraying. With regularity, the male will toss up his hind legs and spray the surrogate mate. This can be comical to other family members but it does increase laundry and dry-cleaning bills.
- Nudging and digging. These are frequent demands for attention coupled with following the selected mate everywhere.
- Imitating the mating act. This sometimes embarrassing trait is performed on legs, arms, elbows, or whatever else happens to be in the way at the time.

I have been told that does behave in a manner similar to a feline in heat. My friend, Cathy, has told me that the female bunny will select a male family member as a surrogate mate and that guests are not exempt from bunny romancing.

In my opinion, the male is a little more difficult to cope with because of the spraying and his aggressive behavior. It is not advisable to spend time with your bunny at floor level during this period unless you enjoy laundry detail.

Finally, Woodstock and I came to an understanding. He wouldn't spray me on the "No-no-no-no-no, Woodstock" command and I wouldn't verbally rebuke or chastise him for doing what is natural.

Woodstock consumed mega quantities of water and greens during the mating season and was frantic during his outings. He performed quantum leaps and his speed made the roadrunner look anemic. He was particularly active at night between 10:00 and 12:00 P.M.

A tip for rabbit owners with children is to adjust your pet's evening outings during the mating season to before or after the children are in bed. You should also have an explanation for the children about the change in your pet's behavior.

What to Do and When to Do It

Do not delay if you are going to have your rabbit (of either sex) neutered. I didn't believe in altering the natural propensities of any pet, but that was B.W. (before Woodstock). Once we had him, it became evident that something had to be done, and this opened a whole new set of circumstances to be considered.

- How do you choose a veterinarian to do the deed?
- How much does it cost? (If you procrastinate as I did, by this time you should have earned shares in your local dry-cleaning company.)

- What do you have to do and what type of post-operative care do you need to provide for the recuperation period?

Here are some guidelines based on my experience with Woodstock:

1. Choose a veterinarian with a known reputation for working with exotic pets. These dedicated people know more about rabbits than veterinarians who see mostly dogs and cats. To find an exotic-pet veterinarian, use your Yellow Pages and ask for referrals from friends. Interview by telephone or personal visit before you make a decision. You will probably find that one or two names are constantly mentioned. Your final choice should be based on your rapport with the vet. Do not hesitate to request references.

2. Understand the neutering process. Woodstock's incision was sealed with surgical glue, a modern technique in veterinary medicine. Animals tend to pull at stitches or metal sutures. Woodstock still managed to reopen his incision but I believe that is unusual for rabbits. Knowing Woodstock, this didn't come as a big surprise.

3. Be certain your pet has had a thorough physical examination before surgery and that you know what type of anesthetic will be used. Woodstock was given

presurgery antibiotics as, taking into consideration postoperative complications, the veterinarian believed in preventative medicine. Woodstock has had two veterinarians care for him and in both cases has had superlative health care and attention.

4. I recommend a tour of the hospital facilities if it can be arranged. That way you will know the standards of housing the clinic or hospital maintains. I would not place my pet in a clinic that did not house rabbits separately under antiseptic conditions.

5. It would be advantageous to have your veterinarian board your rabbit overnight before the surgery and be responsible for its fasting, particularly if you have children. You do not want anyone giving your rabbit treats or unscheduled food, with or without your knowledge.

6. The family member the rabbit has adopted as a surrogate mate should be available during check-in and check-out times. That way your pet will feel less disoriented at these crucial moments. The whole process of having a rabbit neutered should be planned. Keep in mind that a truly user-friendly bunny is created by a strong support system and you cannot afford to have your pet feel abandoned at this time.

7. Be certain that your vet calls you or a designated family member immediately following the operation or recovery so that he or she does not get a number of phone calls. Only one person should be involved and it is a good idea for an adult to take this responsibility in the unlikely event of complications with the surgery.

8. When your rabbit is safely back in its home, give it time to adjust; understand that it has been through a traumatic experience, has been housed in a different cage, has some form of suturing, and will be somewhat uncomfortable. I have been told that rabbits recuperate rapidly but your pet needs a few days of peace and quiet.

9. When you collect your pet, get an emergency number. Be sure to ask the veterinarian when your rabbit was last fed and the last time it urinated. Carefully monitor urine and droppings in the cage for the first two days. If your pet does not urinate or defecate within 24 hours, inform your vet immediately. Always know where you can obtain emergency service. Woodstock did not urinate during the first 24 hours, which alarmed me. Naturally, it was on a weekend. A half dozen calls later, I was at the panic stage. I had arranged for emergency vet service a half an hour drive away, when Woodstock decided the "game was up," proving once again that I overreact.

10. Check your rabbit daily to be certain there is no undue redness around the incision or unusual swelling. This area will have been shaved. Your pet is most easily examined on a high table or counter. If you are managing this by yourself and need both hands for a grip, the fur will part if you blow on it and you can easily inspect the incision while firmly holding your pet.

Post-op Care

Expect your pet's food and water intake to be less than normal for a few days. If offered, fresh greens or carrots should be in less than normal quantity. Dried hay or alfalfa is acceptable. Remove any unconsumed vegetables immediately.

When I picked up Woodstock from the hospital with Petey, he told our vet, "She'll probably kiss all the fur off his head in the next 24 hours." He didn't know how true this was! I was unaware that Stocky's operation had coincided with the shedding season and I was alarmed to find him losing large quantities of fur. His coat was a yellowish color in patches and he was scruffy in appearance. I thought it was related to his stay in the clinic or a result of the operation. I immediately went into my overreact mode until I was assured that it was just the season.

We gave Woodstock his freedom the morning following the operation expecting that as he was "under the weather," he wouldn't leave his cage. However, he came flying out as usual and you would never have known he'd just had surgery. We did not handle Woodstock until he approached us, which was about a week. We figured it took him that long to forgive us for the anatomical adjustment.

We were told that neutering would make him much calmer. Taking this risk seemed better than being a surrogate mate but I was concerned that it might change his personality. However Woodstock remained uniquely Woodstock and, if anything, has become more affectionate to us and more trustworthy around the apartment. He has never sprayed since. He still circles people he adopts but I no longer have to cross my fingers and hope he won't do anything to my guests.

Since neutering tends to remove a certain amount of aggressiveness, responsible rabbit owners should keep a sharp eye on their pets outdoors as they will be less likely to defend themselves vigorously against predators.

Chapter 13

Keeping Your Bunny Healthy*

A properly fed, well-maintained, indoor pet rabbit may not require much more health care than an annual veterinary checkup and regular grooming. However, rabbits kept outdoors or allowed out in the summer, should be examined both in the spring and fall. A stool sample examination should be included to help rule out the presence of internal parasites, and the coat should be examined thoroughly for the presence of external parasites.

Diet and husbandry are key elements in your pet's overall care. This chapter will deal with only those aspects that most commonly lead to health problems.

In terms of health care, the old axiom "an ounce of prevention is worth a pound of cure" still holds. However, when treatment is required, early detection of health problems is essential to a successful outcome. This chapter will outline an easy way for you to examine your rabbit at home, as well as discuss some of the most common health problems encountered.

*This chapter was written by Petra Burgmann, DVM.

Dietary Considerations

Rabbits are extremely prone to digestive disturbances if they are not fed properly. Fresh rabbit pellets should constitute 85 percent of the daily diet. Buying more pellets than can be used in a two-month period is the equivalent of eating two-month-old bread; both the palatability and the nutritive value will be decreased markedly by this time. The pellets you purchase should be a rich green color and smell of fresh hay. Be particularly observant in the late winter and early spring. Often these pellets are produced from hay harvested the year before, and are not as fresh as those available at other times of the year. You may have to go to more than one pet store to find pellets that are as fresh as possible. If your rabbit is refusing to eat the pellets you are providing, purchase a fresh bag; your pet may be aware of something that you are not. If your rabbit's inappetence persists, suspect an underlying health problem as the cause, and seek veterinary care.

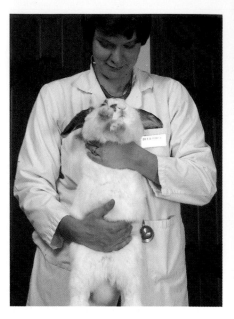

Left: When examining your rabbit, hold its spine against your chest. Right: Slide one hand up, extending the forelegs. Slide the other hand down, causing the rear legs to stretch out.

Alfalfa hay should constitute another 10 percent of the daily diet. Fresh alfalfa hay is preferable to alfalfa cubes because it appears to cause less digestive disturbances. Good quality alfalfa hay is extremely important in the daily diet because it provides roughage necessary to prevent gastric hair balls.

Vegetables and fruits can make up the remaining 5 percent of the daily diet. Carrots, broccoli, spinach, watercress, alfalfa sprouts, bananas, and apples are all good choices. Be careful not to overfeed fresh fruits and vegetables, especially in very young rabbits. Dwarf rabbits under six months of age are especially prone to digestive disturbances, and it is recommended to avoid fresh greens altogether until the rabbit is six months old.

Treat feeding, such as oats, cookies, cereal, or seeds, must be very limited (no more than a teaspoonful a day) to avoid carbohydrate overload to the hindgut.

In terms of your rabbit's overall body condition and weight, this basic rule of thumb can be applied: You should be able to outline your rabbit's ribs and hips with your fingertips, but you should not be able to see the bones across the room. In other words, there should not be a half-inch layer of fat to reach through before you can feel bone, nor a sagging, pot-bellied abdomen, but the spine and space between the hips should not be prominent, nor the eyes sunken in the skull. The coat should be shiny and pliable, and spring back immediately after pinching up an inch with your fingers.

Husbandry Considerations

A clean, well-maintained environment is essential to your pet's well-being. In terms of health care, protection from drafts, chills, dampness, and overheating are important considerations. A dry, raised cage that is placed out of the direct sun and well insulated in the winter is required. There is some controversy as to whether a wire-bottomed or flat-bottomed cage is better for rabbits. I find that this choice must be made on an individual pet basis. Some rabbits are born with thin metatarsal fur pads; these rabbits are prone to developing hock sores (see page 70). For these individuals, a flat-bottomed cage and even a blanket are required to prevent trauma and damage to the delicate metatarsal region. Other rabbits are notorious blanket/wood/paper chewers and must be kept away from these materials. In this case, a wire-bottomed cage is preferable. Still others prefer a wire-bottomed cage with a flat wood "resting area." What is essential to each cage design is that it is made of easy-to-clean, waterproof, nontoxic materials.

Exercise Requirements

Your rabbit should be allowed at least two to three hours of exercise every day. Denying your pet this exercise would be the human equivalent of being locked in a bathroom

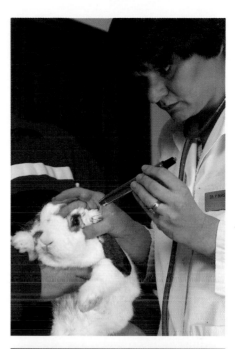

Check the eyes for signs of discharge.

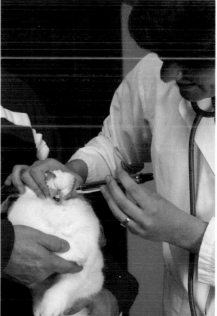

Examine the teeth for curling or uneven wear.

day after day. Adequate exercise is essential in maintaining a healthy, emotionally stable, and well-socialized pet.

Signs of Good Health

Signs of good health include bright eyes, responsive and active behavior, and a good appetite for both pellets and hay.

Fecal pellets should be round, firm, and pea-sized, with similar quantities being produced each day. There is some natural variation in rabbit urine. It may range from clear yellow in color to a cloudy white shade that is filled with crystals. This is a perfectly normal variation and not a cause for concern.

Signs of Health Problems

The following is a list of clinical signs indicating a need for veterinary care. Be sure to choose a veterinarian knowledgeable in rabbit medicine.

- discharge from the eyes or nose
- blue or pale mucous membranes (gums)
- panting when not hot or frightened
- gurgling gas sounds in the abdomen
- excessively hot to touch
- reluctance to eat; either shows in-terest, but appears unable to grasp food, or shows no interest in food
- drooling
- diarrhea
- no fecal pellets passed
- fecal pellets passed are much smaller and harder than usual
- orange, red, or thick cloudy brown urine
- urine scalding around the groin or on the hind legs
- sudden inability to walk
- bald patches
- waxy crusty debris in the ears
- excessively itchy skin
- red scaly skin between the shoulder blades
- sores on the hocks
- any lumps, bumps, or swellings

How to Examine Your Rabbit for Health Problems

The first and most important step in examining your rabbit is to be able to restrain it properly. The secret is to be able to place your pet in a "bunny grip," a holding technique I developed several years ago for restraining rabbits during an office physical examination.

Rabbits have a disproportionate muscle mass to skeletal mass; their muscle mass is much more like a dog's, whereas their skeletal mass is more like a cat's. For this reason, it is easy for a rabbit to kick out suddenly with its hind legs and fracture its spine. Properly restraining a rabbit involves protecting its spine from injury and preventing any sudden kicks.

With the rabbit facing away from you, place both hands under the rabbit's chest and lift the animal, placing its spine against your chest. Slide your left hand up under the rabbit's armpits extending the forelegs up while simultaneously sliding the flat of your right hand down the abdomen, causing the hind legs to stretch out to their full extent. Keep your right hand firmly pressed against the lower abdomen, so the legs cannot draw up towards the body. Make sure the rabbit's spine is kept straight. This grip prevents the rabbit from getting any power in its hind legs to kick suddenly, injuring both itself and you. A second person can now examine the rabbit closely.

Check the eyes and nose for any signs of discharge. Note whether the discharge is clear, white, yellow, green, or brown.

Lift the upper lip and examine the incisors for any signs of curling or uneven wear. The teeth should be white and clean, and all four incisors should be equal in length.

Check inside the ears for any evidence of waxy or crusty debris. Check the upper surface for scaly skin.

Check the body for any lumps, bumps, or swellings. Note whether the abdomen appears distended, or if there is a "sloshing" sound or excessive gurgling when the abdomen is moved from side to side. "Flick" the abdomen gently with your thumb and middle finger; the abdomen should

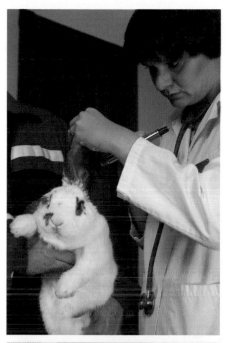

Check the inside of the ear for dirt or excessive wax. Don't try to examine or clean the inside of the canal.

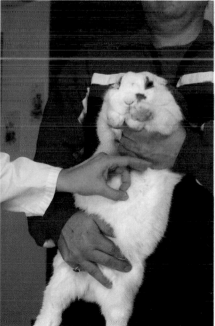

"Flick" a finger against the abdomen to check for gas. You will find a hollow-sounding area in the middle of the right side.

not sound hollow except for a plum-sized patch towards the middle of the right-hand side. This area contains a small pocket of gas that tends to occur naturally in the cecum, a portion of the digestive tract. An excessively large area of gas may indicate the beginning of a digestive disturbance and should be examined more carefully.

Check the toenails for excessive length and trim them if necessary, taking care not to nip the quick (a small blood vessel) present in the nail.

Check the hind end for evidence of diarrhea or urine scalding. Clean or brush out the fur as required, being careful not to tear the delicate skin in this area.

Check the points of the hocks for thin fur pads or any evidence of sores. Never trim the fur pads directly over the points of the hock on a rabbit, even if the fur is soiled. Simply wash the fur with soap and water and rinse thoroughly. Trimming this fur, particularly in angora rabbits, is a common mistake and leads to hock sores.

As you place the rabbit back down on a table, maintaining your grip around its chest, examine the fur for any areas of balding, evidence of external parasites, or areas of red, scaly skin between the shoulder blades.

First Aid Measures

Most of the major health ailments of rabbits require veterinary intervention, but a few simple first aid measures can be performed at home until veterinary care is available.

Minor cuts and abrasions can be cleaned with hydrogen peroxide, which is readily available at your local pharmacy. Simply trim the hair around the injury and apply hydrogen peroxide with a cotton ball to the affected area. Do not use the antiseptic around the eyes.

Overheating, often caused by a rabbit being transported in a hot car or being left in the sun too long without shade, must be treated immediately. Place your rabbit in a cool room and wet its fur with cool water until your pet is breathing more normally.

Inability to grasp food, due to malocclusion or broken incisors, must be dealt with professionally. In order to keep a rabbit eating until help can be sought, mixed vegetable baby food or soaked rabbit pellets can be syringed into the rabbit's mouth two to three times a day at roughly a teaspoonful at a sitting. Care must be taken not to feed too much at a time to prevent choking.

Runny eyes or nose can be wiped with a warm wet cotton ball to prevent buildup of the secretions and damage to the delicate skin around these areas until veterinary advice can be obtained.

Urine scald can be treated by cleaning the affected skin gently but thoroughly with soap and water, taking care to rinse well afterwards. Urine that remains on the delicate skin of the hind quarters for a long time can cause severe skin irritation and sloughing.

Diarrhea should be washed off the hindquarters with soap and water. Always be sure to rinse away soap residue thoroughly. All vegetable, fruit, and treat feeding should be discontinued immediately and fresh water should be available to prevent dehydration. If the diarrhea persists for more than 24 hours, seek veterinary care.

Constipation actually is quite rare in rabbits. More often than not, no stools are being produced because the rabbit has stopped eating. Do not administer a laxative; seek veterinary care.

Bloated abdomen and labored respiration indicate a true emergency situation; Give a half teaspoonful (2–3 cc) of an antiflatulent preparation, such as Diovol Plus, to help break up the gas and seek help immediately.

Common Health Problems

Though the following list of diseases is by no means comprehensive, it does include those most commonly encountered. The purpose of this section is to familiarize you with various diseases rather than to suggest a cure. Treating any condition must take into account the individual pet and the severity of the illness, assessments that are best made by your own veterinarian.

Ear Mites

Rabbits, especially those kept outdoors, are especially prone to the ear mite *Psoroptes cuniculi*. The mite burrows in the skin of the inner ear causing a dry, brown, crusty exudate to form. When this exudate is removed, a moist, red, very painful skin surface is exposed. Rabbits with this condition often shake their heads and scratch at their ears causing self-mutilation. Treatment consists of instilling five to ten drops of plain mineral oil in the ear, waiting several hours for the crusts to soften, then gently wiping out the ear canal with cotton and repeating the process every three days for several weeks until the ear canal is clean and healed. It should be noted, however, that the condition is extremely painful, and in severe cases a general anesthetic and veterinary care may be required. The mite can exist off the host for several weeks, therefore a thorough, repeated disinfecting of the environment is also essential.

Fur Mites

The fur mite *Cheyletiella parasitovorax* is not often referred to in pet care books, but is quite common in veterinary practice. Clinical signs include a thinning of the fur between the shoulder blades, progressing to red scaly skin over the back and head. The mite causes mild to moderate itching in the rabbit, but can also bite people or other pet animals, causing an itch similar to a mosquito bite. Treatment consists of bathing

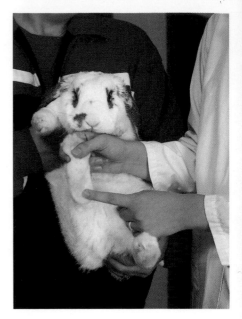

Left: Check the nails and trim if necessary.
Right: Examine the hocks for thin fur or sores.

the rabbit with a mild insecticide shampoo suitable for use on puppies and kittens, then powdering the rabbit lightly with a 5 percent carbaryl insecticide powder. `Insecticides in rabbits can be toxic, so be sure to ask your veterinarian to recommend the products most suitable. Do not buy over-the-counter pet store products for this purpose, as many of them are too toxic for rabbits.

Pasteurellosis

Pasteurellosis is a bacterial infection caused by the organism *Pasteurella multocida.* It is estimated that as much as 85 percent of rabbits carry the organism in their nasal passages naturally, but given certain stress

conditions, or in the weaker very young or very old animal, the condition can progress to cause obvious disease. The most common occurrence is a rabbit with one chronically runny eye or nasal discharge. The infection can progress to cause pneumonia and abscesses in the jaw or elsewhere in the body, or it can affect the inner ear causing a head tilt. Severe cases can cause a generalized septicemia, resulting in fever and lethargy, and may bring about the death of the animal. Mild ocular discharge from one eye often can be treated locally with eye drops alone, but pneumonia or inner ear infections must be treated with oral or injectable antibiotics. It is important to be aware

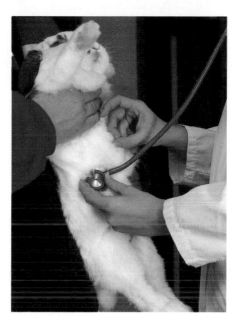

Left: Check the skin and coat for parasites, hair loss, and any signs of irritation.

Right: Regular visits to your veterinarian will help keep your pet healthy.

that treatment of this condition seldom will result in a complete cure. Rather, the aim of therapy is to reduce the infection back to its subclinical form so that the rabbit no longer is in discomfort. Pasteurellosis is a serious condition in rabbits that requires veterinary intervention.

Digestive Upset

Digestive upset is a general term used to describe a wide variety of gastrointestinal conditions in rabbits, including bloat and diarrhea.

Bloat occurs because rabbits have an extremely sensitive bacterial flora in the intestine. Any disruption in the normal balance of the bacterial organisms present in the bowel, due to improper diet or to a change in intestinal motility, can cause the wrong kind of bacteria to multiply, resulting in excess gas production. The excess gas produced distends the bowel, causing further disruption in intestinal motility. In the worst cases it can cause the bowel to rupture. Certain kinds of bacteria can release toxins into the bloodstream affecting other organ systems.

Diarrhea also can be caused by certain bacterial organisms, or by intestinal parasites such as coccidia, a protozoal parasite.

Severe gastrointestinal disturbances can result in death, and are more easily avoided than cured. Most gastrointestinal disturbances are caused by improper feeding habits. Following the dietary recommendations given previously in this chapter will prevent most of these disturbances. If severe bloat or diarrhea are present, veterinary care should be sought immediately. Be sure to take a stool sample along for the veterinarian to examine.

Gastric Hair Balls

Rabbits are especially prone to developing gastric hair balls for two reasons. They lack the natural ability to vomit, and the opening from their stomach to their intestine is relatively small; therefore, it is very hard for them to get rid of hair or rug fibers that accumulate in their stomach. Owners most often notice that even though their pet appears bright and alert, the rabbit eats less and less food and produces progressively smaller, harder stools than normal. Many rabbits stop eating their pelleted feed first, then their hay, and then their greens, so that the progression of the illness can be so subtle that the owner may not be aware of the problem until the hair ball is quite large, occupying most of the stomach lumen. This condition can be very difficult to treat, and veterinary care is essential to correct the condition.

Bladder Infections

Though bladder infections are not common in rabbits, they do occur. In a bladder infection frank blood or red urine will be seen. This condition will require treatment with an appropriate antibiotic.

Orange urine, however, does not indicate a bladder infection. Orange urine is produced when porphyrin pigment is excreted in the urine. This can occur during stress, when there is water deprivation, of if the diet contains high levels of certain minerals or pigments. If water deprivation is not the cause, the occasional production of orange urine is not a cause for concern. However, if the pigmented urine is produced for several days in a row, the cause should be identified and eliminated.

Hock Sores

Hock sores is a condition in which there are open sores or ulcers on the plantar surface of the hind feet. This occurs when the fur pad covering the area below the point of the hock is insufficient to protect the area from damage. There are four basic causes of this condition: the cage floor surface is too rough; the fur is soiled allowing it to become matted; the fur pad is thin from birth; or the fur pad has been trimmed away by an overly enthusiastic grooming by the owner. It is important that no further trauma occur to the hock so that healing can take place. Removing the wire bottom of the cage, padding the resting area with towels, (make sure that the rabbit does not ingest the towel), or, in some cases, bandaging the area will permit healing. Severe cases may progress to a deep pus filled sore that can result in a septic arthritis of the joints, and should be treated with an appropriate antibiotic.

Fractures

The two most common fractures are those of the spine and the forelegs. The forelegs often fracture when a rabbit is allowed to climb up the front of the owner and then catapult over the owner's shoulder onto the floor. These fractures can often be repaired surgically.

Spinal fractures can occur anytime a rabbit kicks out suddenly with its hind legs, such as during handling or even strenuous play. If the spine is just dislocated, the rabbit may recover with intensive medical care. If the spine is fractured, no medical treatment will be of much help and euthanasia should be considered.

Myxomatosis

Myxomatosis is caused by a virus transmitted by insect bite or contact with infected cage wire. It is more common in the western United States, Europe and Australia than elsewhere in the world. The infection ranges from a mild form which causes fibromas, to a severe form which causes red skin, swollen eyelids, purulent conjunctivitis, and jelly-like swellings under the skin of the face, ears and genitals. Death usually occurs 8 to 12 days following exposure. In rabbits that survive, the lesions usually fade within three months. No treatment is known. The best advice is to prevent exposure by keeping pets in an insect proof enclosure and preventing contact with wild rabbits.

Chapter 14
Travelbunny

Woodstock has traveled with me in everything from a nylon sports shoulder bag to an airline travel cage to my purse. Before I received delivery of a custom-designed travel cage,(see photo page 18), I took him in the summer to visit a friend about an hour's drive out of town. He was loose in the car and since our back seats fold down, he elected to hide himself at the furthest corner, which was in the trunk. Despite air conditioning, the temperature must have been at least 80° F (25° C). I discovered that he will always go to the furthest corner of my car and flop.

My friends have two rabbits that travel everywhere with them in their van and none of us have ever had an experience where our pets have interfered with the safe operation of a motor vehicle. Bunnies seem to follow a set of bunny rules when loose in a car or van. Given a choice, they normally avoid anything that could be injurious to their health. However, you should check for open windows, extreme temperatures, doors ajar, open containers of harmful substances, loose plastic bags or caps, or antifreeze. You should be particularly aware of any electrical wiring your pet may be tempted to nibble on in the course of your trip.

Travel Housing

I would recommend a travel cage similar to the one in the photo on page 18. In this type of cage, the lower drawer is used for supplies such as pellets, harness and lead, and plastic bags or containers of fresh greens. This enables you to put all your pet's needs in one place. If your bunny is going to be away for more than a day, I suggest an open wire cage as opposed to the vinyl enclosed type which I only use for short outings such as a trip to the veterinarian's office.

When traveling with my rabbit either loose or in a cage, I always have him harnessed. This enables me to clip him easily to a lead upon arrival and to have control over his safety should he become disoriented.

Destination Housing

Regardless of where you are taking your pet, have four carpet-type

After a long afternoon in the park, Woodstock is ready to get into his travel case and return home.

mats that you can put in the four corners of whatever space your rabbit will be offered. If you have kept your original training mats they will still have your pet's stake-out scent on them and your bunny may not get the urge to mark its territory in your friend's living room. It is also a good idea to take along your rabbit's training tray and place it on top of the mat in the furthest corner diagonally from where you position the travel cage.

Understand that your rabbit may want to stake out its new environment, which is why you should protect your friends' home with the mats. If your pet is completely housebroken you should have no cause for concern. Establish in advance what area is going to be allocated for bunny antics and stick to it. Do not permit anyone to take your pet out of the area without warning them that it may decide to stake out the new territory. It is not recommended that you take your rabbit to visit friends who have a dog or a cat unless you are willing to risk your friendship.

It is important to purchase a travel cage that is spacious enough for your rabbit to turn around and stretch out in. Bus lines, railways, and airlines have regulations about cage sizes to house traveling animals. This is for humane reasons. These standards can provide you with guidelines if you are uncertain about what size travel cage to purchase for your rabbit, and the information is readily available with a telephone call.

When traveling with your rabbit, know that strangers will want to approach you and handle your pet. As mentioned in Outdoor Training, give instructions before handing your pet to anyone.

Afterword:
The Mature Rabbit

The mature rabbit is the most gratifying and loving pet you could wish for. Love and compassion are the only ingredients needed for a totally rewarding experience.

Accidentally, I discovered that the rabbit's learning curve seems to be limitless. I have offered the advice contained in this book to people who have been given mature rabbits and in all cases the feedback has been positive.

The rabbit's ability to adapt to its surroundings is quite astonishing. Woodstock is now a mature rabbit and has been exposed to TV lights and cameras, has been handled by literally hundreds of people, and, although I suspect he is a natural ham, he seems to take everything in his stride.

As you will discover, rabbits can be quite comical and, as they are still an unusual house pet, sometimes disconcerting to your guests. The mature rabbit can be counted on to respond on command, be friendly and trusting, be good with children and senior citizens, and to be an interesting companion.

I believe in the truth of the statement, "You're nobody 'til some bunny loves you!"

Useful Addresses and Literature

Periodicals
Domestic Rabbits (monthly)
The American Rabbit Breeders Association
1925 South Main, Box 426
Bloomington, IL 81701

Rabbits (monthly)
Countryside Publication, Ltd.
312 Portland Road, Highway 19 East
Waterloo, WI 53594

Books
The American Rabbit Breeders Association, *Official Guide to Raising Better Rabbits,* Bloomington, Illinois.

Sandford, J.C. *The Domestic Rabbit*, Collins, London, 1986
Wegler, Monika, *Dwarf Rabbits*, Barron's Hauppauge, New York, 1986
——, *Rabbits,* Barron's, Hauppauge, New York, 1990.
Vriends-Parent, Lucia, *The New Rabbit Handbook,* Barron's, Hauppauge, New York, 1989.

Index

Perfect for Pet Owners!

PET OWNER'S MANUALS

Over 50 illustrations per book (20 or more color photos), 72–80 pp., paperback.

ABYSSINIAN CATS
AFRICAN GRAY PARROTS
AMAZON PARROTS
BANTAMS
BEAGLES
BEEKEEPING
BOSTON TERRIERS
BOXERS
CANARIES
CATS
CHINCHILLAS
CHOW-CHOWS
CICHLIDS
COCKATIELS
COCKER SPANIELS
COCKATOOS
COLLIES
CONURES
DACHSHUNDS
DALMATIANS
DISCUS FISH
DOBERMAN PINSCHERS
DOGS
DOVES
DWARF RABBITS
ENGLISH SPRINGER SPANIELS
FEEDING AND SHELTERING BACKYARD
    BIRDS
FEEDING AND SHELTERING EUROPEAN
    BIRDS
FERRETS
GERBILS
GERMAN SHEPHERDS
GOLDEN RETRIEVERS
GOLDFISH
GOULDIAN FINCHES
GREAT DANES
GUINEA PIGS
GUPPIES, MOLLIES, AND PLATTIES
HAMSTERS
HEDGEHOGS
IRISH SETTERS
KEESHONDEN
KILLIFISH
LABRADOR RETRIEVERS
LHASA APSOS
LIZARDS IN THE TERRARIUM
LONGHAIRED CATS

LONG-TAILED PARAKEETS
LORIES AND LORIKEETS
LOVEBIRDS
MACAWS
MICE
MUTTS
MYNAHS
PARAKEETS
PARROTS
PERSIAN CATS
PIGEONS
POMERANIANS
PONIES
POODLES
POT BELLIES AND OTHER MINIATURE PIGS
PUGS
RABBITS
RATS
ROTTWEILERS
SCHNAUZERS
SCOTTISH FOLD CATS
SHAR-PEI
SHEEP
SHETLAND SHEEPDOGS
SHIH TZUS
SIAMESE CATS
SIBERIAN HUSKIES
SMALL DOGS
SNAKES
SPANIELS
TROPICAL FISH
TURTLES
WEST HIGHLAND WHITE TERRIERS
YORKSHIRE TERRIERS
ZEBRA FINCHES

NEW PET HANDBOOKS

Detailed, illustrated profiles (40–60 color photos), 144 pp., paperback.

NEW AQUARIUM FISH HANDBOOK
NEW AUSTRALIAN PARAKEET
    HANDBOOK
NEW BIRD HANDBOOK
NEW CANARY HANDBOOK
NEW CAT HANDBOOK
NEW COCKATIEL HANDBOOK
NEW DOG HANDBOOK
NEW DUCK HANDBOOK
NEW FINCH HANDBOOK

NEW GOAT HANDBOOK
NEW PARAKEET HANDBOOK
NEW PARROT HANDBOOK
NEW RABBIT HANDBOOK
NEW SALTWATER AQUARIUM
    HANDBOOK
NEW SOFTBILL HANDBOOK
NEW TERRIER HANDBOOK

REFERENCE BOOKS

Comprehensive, lavishly illustrated references (60–300 color photos), 136–176 pp., hardcover & paperback.

AQUARIUM FISH
AQUARIUM FISH BREEDING
AQUARIUM FISH SURVIVAL MANUAL
AQUARIUM PLANTS MANUAL
BEFORE YOU BUY THAT PUPPY
BEST PET NAME BOOK EVER, THE
CARING FOR YOUR SICK CAT
CAT CARE MANUAL
CIVILIZING YOUR PUPPY
COMMUNICATING WITH YOUR DOG
COMPLETE BOOK OF BUDGERIGARS
COMPLETE BOOK OF CAT CARE
COMPLETE BOOK OF DOG CARE
DOG CARE MANUAL
FEEDING YOUR PET BIRD
GOLDFISH AND ORNAMENTAL CARP
GUIDE TO A WELL-BEHAVED CAT
GUIDE TO HOME PET GROOMING
HEALTHY CAT, HAPPY CAT
HEALTHY DOG, HAPPY DOG
HOP TO IT: A Guide to Training Your Pet
    Rabbit
HORSE CARE MANUAL
HOW TO TALK TO YOUR CAT
HOW TO TEACH YOUR OLD DOG
    NEW TRICKS
LABYRINTH FISH
NONVENOMOUS SNAKES
TROPICAL MARINE FISH
    SURVIVAL MANUAL

Barron's Educational Series, Inc. • 250 Wireless Blvd., Hauppauge, NY 11788
Call toll-free: 1-800-645-3476 • In Canada: Georgetown Book Warehouse
34 Armstrong Ave., Georgetown, Ont. L7G 4R9 • Call toll-free: 1-800-247-7160
Order from your favorite book or pet store.

(#62) R 2/97